4-05

P9-CFT-340

MONSON FREE LIBRARY
MONSON, MA 01057

JOHANNES KEPLER
DISCOVERING THE LAWS
OF CELESTIAL MOTION

JOHANNES KEPLER
DISCOVERING THE LAWS
OF CELESTIAL MOTION

William J. Boerst

MORGAN
REYNOLDS
Publishing, Inc.

620 South Elm Street, Suite 223
Greensboro, North Carolina   27406
http://www.morganreynolds.com

RENAISSANCE SCIENTISTS

Nicholas Copernicus

Tycho Brahe

Johannes Kepler

Galileo Galilei

Isaac Newton

JOHANNES KEPLER
DISCOVERING THE LAWS OF CELESTIAL MOTION

Copyright © 2003 by William J. Boerst

All rights reserved.
This book, or parts thereof, may not be reproduced in any form
except by written consent of the publisher. For more information write:
Morgan Reynolds Publishing, Inc., 620 South Elm Street, Suite 223
Greensboro, North Carolina 27406 USA

Library of Congress Cataloging-in-Publication Data

Boerst, William J.
    Johannes Kepler : discovering the laws of celestial motion / William
J. Boerst.— 1st ed.
        p. cm. — (Renaissance scientists)
    Summary: A biography of Johannes Kepler, the seventeenth-century German
    astronomer and mathematician who formulated the three laws of planetary
    motion.
    Includes bibliographical references and index.
        ISBN 1-883846-98-6 (lib. bdg.)
        1. Kepler, Johannes, 1571-1630—Juvenile literature. 2.
    Astronomers—Germany—Biography—Juvenile literature. 3. Kepler's
    laws—Juvenile literature. 4. Planetary theory—Juvenile literature.
    [1. Kepler, Johannes, 1571-1630. 2. Astronomers.] I. Title. II. Series.

    QB36.K4B636 2003
    520'.92—dc21

                            2003000708

Printed in the United States of America
First Edition

To Betsy,
whose determination is legendary.

Special thanks to Professor Owen Gingerich for providing information and pictures relevant to the manuscript.

Contents

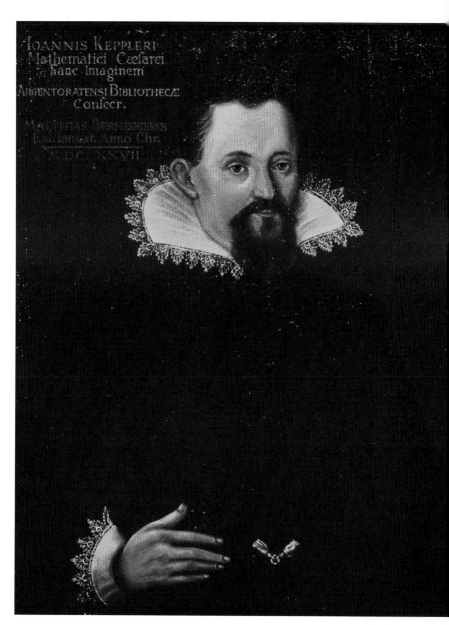

Johannes Kepler, 1627.
(Erich Lessing / Art Resource, NY.)

CHAPTER ONE
RETREAT INTO STUDIES

German astronomer Johannes Kepler was convinced the planets made music as they orbited the Sun. He believed the planets, in conjunction with the Sun and the Moon, were a heavenly orchestra that made a music so beautiful and harmonious it could only be heard by God. Although we on Earth could never hear the music of the spheres, we could use mathematics to understand the laws that governed this perfect harmony.

Kepler based this theory of harmony on the work of the ancient Greek philosopher Pythagoras and his followers, who had discovered a simple set of numerical ratios that explained how to combine musical notes into harmonies. Like Pythagoras, Kepler was convinced there was a similar set of ratios that defined the movements of the heavenly bodies. Kepler called this idea "world harmony," and his lifelong attempt to understand its inner workings led to the discovery of his three laws of planetary motion. These laws provided theoretical support for the idea of a Sun-centered universe and a moving Earth, and became a critical part of modern astronomy.

This woodcut depicts Pythagoras verifying the numerical relationship between the notes of the musical scale. In the upper left-hand picture, the sound of the blacksmiths' hammers inspires the quest to find the ratio. In the upper right-hand picture, Pythagoras tests the sounds produced from glasses of water filled in increments representing the whole numbers 4, 6, 8, 9, 12, and 16. The bottom pictures show him testing the same numbers on weighted strings *(left)* and pipes of varying length *(right)*. *(From Franchino Gafori,* Theorica musice, *Milan, 1492.)*

Martin Luther began the Protestant Reformation when he posted his ninety-five theses on the door of the local church.
(Courtesy of the Library of Congress.)

Kepler searched the heavens for celestial harmony because he lived his life within the disharmony created by the religious conflict that began in 1517, when the German monk and teacher Martin Luther posted a list of ninety-five complaints against the Catholic Church on the door of the local castle church. In this, the first step of what came to be known as the Protestant Reformation, Luther also attacked some of the fundamental beliefs of the Catholic Church.

There had been earlier protests against the monolithic church, but Luther's was the first to spread rapidly. Within a few years, the Protestant Reformation had split Christian Europe into bitterly opposed groups. Over the next decades, periods of uneasy peace were interrupted by sudden religious violence. Arguments about God and

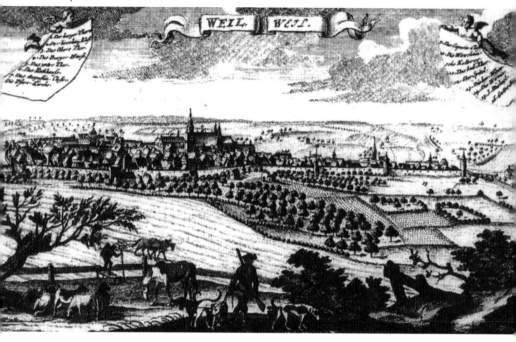

Kepler was born in the imperial city of Weil der Stadt, Germany.
(Courtesy of the Landesbildstelle Württemberg, Stuttgart.)

salvation—who was saved and who was damned—filled public squares and Sunday sermons. Maybe it was this tense environment that prompted Kepler, a brilliant and sensitive young student, to become enchanted with the idea of harmony.

Kepler was born in Weil der Stadt, a city located in the German principality of Württemberg, on December 27, 1571. He was a precocious boy in a tumultuous family. The Keplers had once been part of the nobility, but over the generations their wealth and property had dwindled away. Kepler's grandfather Sebald Kepler had given up his title so that he could legally work as a furrier. Sebald was an ambitious and determined man who served briefly as mayor of Weil der Stadt and had converted to Lutheranism during the first years of the Reformation. Johannes described him as "remarkably arrogant . . . short-tempered and obstinate," and his grandmother as "restless, clever, and lying, but devoted to religion." Toward his mother, Katherine, he also showed little mercy. He wrote she was "small, thin, swarthy, gossiping, and quarrelsome, [and] of a bad disposition."

In 1588, Johannes's father, whom he described as "vicious, inflexible, quarrelsome, and doomed to a bad end," deserted the family to become a mercenary, or a paid soldier, in Italy. Grandfather Sebald became the head of the family. By this time, the Keplers had left Weil der Stadt, which had a predominantly Catholic population, and after a series of moves, finally settled in the Protestant town of Leonberg.

Johannes was the oldest child. Katherine bore six more children, only three of whom survived childhood. Johannes's brother Heinrich, who was two years younger, suffered from epilepsy. Heinrich met with accidents at every turn, and acquaintances and employers frequently abused him. He was beaten, bitten by animals, nearly drowned, and almost burned to death. At age fourteen, Heinrich was apprenticed to a weaver, then to a baker. When his father threatened to sell him, he ran away to Austria and fought against the Turks. Johannes was closer to his sister Margarete and brother Christopher.

Johannes took after his mother in looks and personality. He was thin with a large face and dark, curly hair. His vision was poor, his stomach and gall bladder frequently acted up, his skin was subject to boils and rashes, and he had hemorrhoids, a malady he would endure for his entire life.

He found solace from these physical ailments and his unhappy home life in religion and books. By an early age, his intelligence was obvious to everyone. When the family moved from Weil der Stadt, they were able to take advantage of the educational opportunities provided for boys by the Württemberg dukes, who, after converting to Lutheranism, had created one of the best educational systems in Germany. Their goal was to develop well-educated clergymen, and young Johannes was just the type of boy they had in mind. He was both highly intelligent and deeply religious. He first entered a school where the instruction was given in German, but soon so outpaced the other students and the teachers that he was sent to a Latin school to prepare for the university. He learned to read, write, and speak Latin, which was the language of instruction and educated discourse throughout Europe. His instruction in Latin was so thorough that for the rest of his life his Latin prose was clear and beautiful, while his German was often clumsy and confused.

Despite his obvious intelligence, the chaos in the Kepler household slowed Johannes's progress at school. He lost one year when his father returned to Germany and temporarily relocated the family in a nearby village before leaving again, this time for good. He lost another year when his grandfather decided Johannes had re-

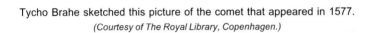

Tycho Brahe sketched this picture of the comet that appeared in 1577.
(Courtesy of The Royal Library, Copenhagen.)

ceived enough education and put him to work washing dishes at an inn he owned. But Johannes was simply too gifted to be left to manual labor. His teachers intervened and Sebald allowed his grandson to return to the school.

Johannes was first introduced to astronomy one night in 1577. His mother woke him and took him to a nearby hillside, where they viewed a comet that had appeared in the heavens a few weeks before. (Hundreds of miles to the north, the Danish astronomer Tycho Brahe, who would later play a critical role in Kepler's life, was busy measuring the comet's progress.) On another night in 1580, she took him out under a clear sky to watch a lunar eclipse.

At the Latin school in Leonberg, Johannes prepared for a career as a clergyman in the Lutheran Church. He continued to excel in Latin, enjoyed writing poetry, and mastered the classics of literature and philosophy. He did sometimes have trouble focusing on the work at hand. He was notorious for bouncing from one topic to

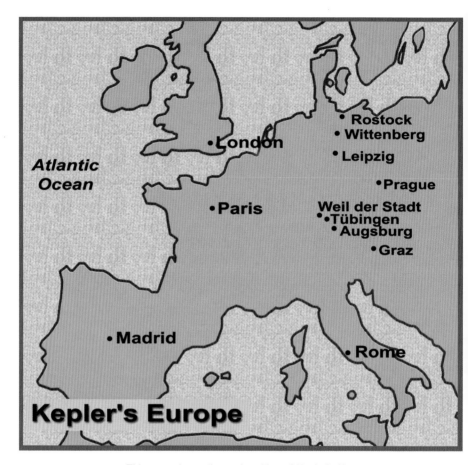

Kepler's Europe

This map shows the major cities of Kepler's Europe.

another in his essays and in his conversations and sometimes made rash comments that seemed intended to shock his listeners. These character traits did not always endear him to his teachers or to the other students.

Johannes was also fiercely competitive. Nothing angered and grieved him more than to think another boy had bested him in a class. Occasionally, his outbursts resulted in fistfights. In his memories of school, he recorded such unhappy events as "I was beaten," and "I have often incensed everyone against me through my own fault."

Sometimes he seemed consumed with self-hatred and developed strange fixations. When he was sixteen years old, he became obsessed with his physical ailments and kept a running list of them. He discovered a worm in the middle finger of his right hand, and a large sore on his left hand also intrigued him. At nineteen, he recorded the development and progress of a long-term fever, cataloged a series of headaches and skin inflammations, and measured his hair loss. He made these observations with remarkable detachment. He even wrote about himself in the third person, which may have made it easier for him to reveal the depth of his self-contempt:

> That man [Kepler] has in every way a dog-like nature. His appearance is that of a little lap-dog. His body is agile, wiry and well-proportioned. Even his appetites were alike. He liked gnawing bones and dry crusts of bread, and was so greedy that whatever his eyes chanced on he grabbed; yet, like a dog, he drinks little and is content with the simplest food ... He continually sought the goodwill of others, was dependent on others for everything, ministered to their wishes, never got angry when they reproved him and was anxious to get back into their favor. He was constantly on the move, ferreting among the sciences, politics and private affairs, including the lowest kind; always following someone else, and imitating his thoughts and actions. He is bored with conversation, but greets

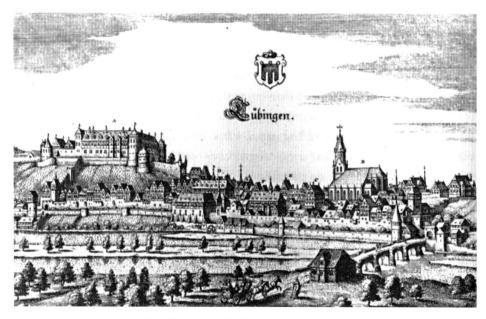

Kepler entered the University of Tübingen to pursue a master's degree in theology.
(Courtesy of the New York Public Library.)

visitors just like a little dog; yet when the least thing is snatched away from him, he flares up and growls. He tenaciously persecutes wrong-doers—that is, he barks at them. He is malicious and bites people with his sarcasms. He hates many people exceedingly and they avoid him, but his masters are fond of him. He has a dog-like horror of baths, tinctures and lotions. His recklessness knows no limits.

Johannes did occasionally list out some of his more positive characteristics, including his "vast appetite for the greatest things," his religious faith, and his willingness to work hard.

In October 1584, at age thirteen, Johannes enrolled

in the Adelberg convent school to continue his clerical training. He was given free room and board; he had finally escaped the Kepler household. In November 1586, he moved on to the higher seminary called Maulbronn. The schedule there was exhaustive. He rose at 4:00 A.M. in summer months, 5:00 A.M. in winter, and began the day by singing psalms. The mandatory uniform was a sleeveless cloak that reached below the knees. In addition to Latin, he took a full course of Greek and read the classic authors Cicero, Virgil, Xenophon, Plato, Aristotle, and Demosthenes in their original language. He also studied rhetoric (the art of speaking and writing effectively), dialectics (reasoning through dialogue), music, and mathematics, which included astronomy. Kepler needed to excel in order to continue receiving scholarships. He was intellectually confident, however, and not afraid to voice his opposition to an idea or theory held by the majority or by his teachers.

In September 1588, Johannes passed his baccalaureate examination, but he had to return for another year at Maulbronn before entering the University of Tübingen to work toward a master's degree in theology. In exchange for attending Tübingen and receiving a stipend, room, board, and tuition, Kepler agreed to work in the Lutheran Church under the direction of the duke of Württemberg for the rest of his life. This meant he would serve at the pleasure of the duke and would have to receive permission before he could change his career or move away from Württemberg.

Michael Maestlin became Kepler's teacher and mentor at the University of Tübingen. *(Courtesy of Owen Gingerich.)*

He began studying at the University of Tübingen in September 1589, where he took more classes in Latin, Greek, rhetoric, Hebrew, and religion. He continued to excel in these courses, but increasingly mathematics, which included astronomy, commanded his attention. The late sixteenth century was an exciting time to study astronomy, and Kepler was fortunate that one of Europe's most respected teachers taught at the University of Tübingen. Michael Maestlin had written a widely used astronomy textbook and corresponded with most of the major professional and amateur astronomers in Europe.

Maestlin's textbook was based on the theories of Claudius Ptolemy, a Greek mathematician and astronomer who had lived in Alexandria, Egypt, during the second century A.D. Ptolemy developed a planetary system based on the ideas of the fourth-century-B.C. Greek philosopher Aristotle, who established a set of laws for physics and astronomy that held sway for nearly two thousand years. He wrote that the world was made of four elements—earth, fire, water, and air—and that there was a fifth element, aether, in the heavens. According to Aristotle, Earth was composed of the heaviest elements, and it naturally came to rest in the center of the universe. The Sun circled Earth, as did the other planets. There was one set of physical laws for Earth and another set for the celestial realm beyond the Moon.

Aristotle wrote the celestial sphere, which stretched from the Moon to the outer sphere of stars, was composed of the single element aether. In the middle ages, philosophers fashioned this aether into crystalized spheres that controlled planetary orbits. The planets, Sun, and Moon traveled around the stationary Earth in uniform circular motion.

Following the teachings of Aristotle, Ptolemy developed a model of the universe that attempted to systemize Aristotle's philosophy. There were problems with this model though. The word planet itself comes from the Greek word for "wanderer," and that's exactly what they seemed to do. The planets did not adhere to the three principles of Ptolemy's model.

In his work that came to be known by its Arabic title *Almagest,* Ptolemy attempted to solve the problem of the unruly planets by creating an epicyclical system. Planets followed a small orbit called an epicycle that in turn orbited in a bigger sphere called a deferent. This system of circles was used to predict planetary positions.

Yet, even with epicycles and deferents, the planets did not orbit uniformly from the perspective of Earth. To compensate, Ptolemy created a point in space for each planet, called an equant, from which the planets seemed to move in uniform circular motion. Ptolemy's use of the equant was his biggest deviation from Aristotle.

Over the centuries, Aristotle's physics and Ptolemy's astronomy were incorporated into the Christian worldview. Maestlin taught it to his younger students and used it as the basis for his textbook. Outside of the classroom, however, he advocated the more recent theory of Nicholas Copernicus, a Polish canon, who died in

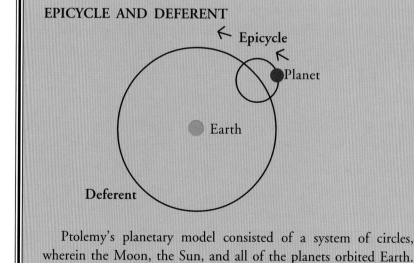

EPICYCLE AND DEFERENT

Ptolemy's planetary model consisted of a system of circles, wherein the Moon, the Sun, and all of the planets orbited Earth. In the simplified diagram above, the large circle represents the deferent and the smaller circle represents the epicycle.

1543. Copernicus spent a great deal of his life developing a heliocentric, or Sun-centered, system, in which Earth and the other known planets orbited around the Sun. Copernicus also believed that Earth spun on its axis once a day.

Copernicus was not the first to suggest a heliocentric universe. The Greek writer Aristarchus proposed the idea in the third century B.C., but it was rejected by the followers of Aristotle. It is easy to see why. The notion of a Sun-centered universe went against common sense. How could Earth orbit the Sun while also spinning daily at such a dizzying rate of speed? What kept objects from flying off into space? If Earth were spinning on an axis, why did a dropped object fall straight down and not at an angle? Why was there no perceptible change in the stars' size and brightness as Earth swirled in its orbit? (Copernicus partly answered this last point by hinting that the universe was so expansive, and the stars so far away, that Earth's orbit was too insignificant to cause a change in the star's size or illumination.)

What the heliocentric model did provide, however, were answers to several nagging questions about planetary motion. For example, one of the most confusing planets had always been Mars, which has one of the most eccentric orbits of all the planets. (Eccentricity refers to the degree an orbit deviates from a circular pattern.) To an observer from Earth, Mars usually moves eastward in its orbit. Occasionally, it seems to stop, back up (move westward), stop again, then proceed eastward. Ptolemy's epicycle system had been designed to explain this retrograde motion.

In Copernicus's system, retrograde motion was explained as the result of Earth's relative motion. Earth is the third planet from the Sun; Mars is the fourth. This means Earth has the "inside track" and travels a shorter orbit. When Earth and Mars are on the same side of the Sun, Earth "laps" Mars. The retrograde motion of Mars is an optical illusion.

Although it answered several questions, there were plenty of problems with Copernicus's system. Because of his insistence on uniform motion and circular orbits, two problems that Kepler would later clear up, Copernicus still relied on epicycles. In addition, he did not answer the physical questions posed by a moving Earth. He had, however, begun the debate that slowly grew to dominate astronomy in the seventeenth century.

Copernicus had been dead for fifty years when Kepler was introduced to his ideas as a student at Tübingen. At the time, Kepler was looking forward to a life serving the Lutheran Church. Other religious men, specifically Protestants, rejected Copernicus. Martin Luther wrote scornfully of the Polish canon who had attempted to turn astronomy on its head. Kepler, however, quickly became convinced that Copernicus was right. He would never waver from that belief for the remainder of his life.

Kepler became a Copernican for a combination of reasons. As he studied Copernicus's book, *On the Revolution of the Celestial Spheres*, he saw that it was a difficult, mathematically sophisticated text. It clearly was not the ruminations of a bored, imaginative man, but the dedicated work of a brilliant and educated mathematician and astronomer. The Copernican model also appealed to him on religious grounds. Kepler had long been convinced that the Sun was God's most brilliant celestial creation. He had first encountered the idea that the Sun was the source of all planetary motion in the works of the Greek philosopher Plato. Although Plato was not a Christian, it seemed right to Kepler that Earth would orbit God's most magnificent creation. It was self-centered of mankind to think God would place Earth in the center of his creation.

Kepler was also convinced the force that drove the planets along their orbits came from the Sun. To Kepler, the Sun represented God. This faith in the Sun would play a critical role in his later discoveries.

Nicholas Copernicus introduced a model of the solar system that featured a central Sun orbited by all the planets. *(Courtesy of the District Museum, Torun.)*

During this time, other discoveries eroded confidence in Aristotle's writings. Tycho Brahe had made extensive observations and measurements of the same comet that had enchanted Kepler as a child in 1577. He had also studied and written about a new star that had appeared in the sky in 1572. In both works, Tycho concluded that change—the birth or death of a new star, the appearance or disappearance of a comet—occurred beyond the Moon, where Aristotle had said no change was possible. Tycho's work on the comet, which traveled across the planets' orbits in a non-circular motion, also undercut Aristotle's claim that the planets rode upon crystalline spheres.

During his last two years at the seminary in Tübingen, Kepler emerged as a gifted mathematician. He was attracted to the subject because of its intellectual challenge, but it also offered an escape from the theological

John Calvin challenged the beliefs of Martin Luther and his followers. *(Courtesy of the Bibliothèque Nationale, Giraudon.)*

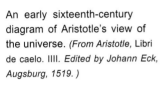

An early sixteenth-century diagram of Aristotle's view of the universe. *(From Aristotle, Libri de caelo. IIII. Edited by Johann Eck, Augsburg, 1519.)*

discussions that usually disintegrated into squabbling and took up so much time at the seminary. The issues extended beyond the tension between Protestants and Catholics as new divisions developed among Protestants. The followers of Martin Luther disagreed with the followers of John Calvin of France, who had set up a church in Geneva, Switzerland, that controlled the city. These arguments were over precise, even minute, aspects of theology that Kepler believed were not central to the main message of Christianity. By his last year at Tübingen, he wondered aloud why it was so difficult to find common ground.

It may have been Kepler's inclination toward reconciliation, as well as his mathematical talent, that caused him to make the great detour of his life. Early in 1594, as he prepared to finish his last months at school and enter the clergy, he was shocked to learn that he had been selected by his teachers to leave his native Germany and travel to Graz, in the Styria district of present day Austria, to teach mathematics at a small seminary.

To accept the position would end his dream of becoming a minister, and Kepler was ambivalent about the appointment. He had prepared for years to enter the clergy and had never considered an alternative career. He did love mathematics and astronomy, but a mathematics teacher in distant Styria would earn a much smaller salary and hold a much less prestigious position than a clergyman in Württemberg. He remained undecided about making the move until Maestlin appealed to him to take the teaching job, arguing that to not do so would be a waste of his talents.

Kepler accepted the position with the stipulation that he could return to clerical studies at a later time. After reaching this agreement, he appealed to the duke of Württemberg for permission to leave his service. The duke granted him permission, and twenty-two-year-old Johannes Kepler borrowed fifty gulden to meet traveling expenses and left for Graz on March 13, 1594.

CHAPTER TWO
COSMOLOGICAL MYSTERY

Kepler turned twenty-three soon after arriving in Graz. Built on a hill and surrounded by a high fortress, Graz was a beautiful town in the southern region of Austria that would soon be ripped apart by religious tension.

During Kepler's lifetime, Germany and most of central Europe was governed by the Holy Roman Empire—a loose confederation of republics and principalities scattered across Central Europe. The emperor was elected by the Reichstag, a governing body that consisted of dozens of princes and nobles. Since 1453, the Catholic Hapsburg family had wielded enough power to control the Reichstag elections, which ensured that a family member was always emperor.

In the beginning of the Protestant Reformation, Martin Luther had been successful in attracting the support of the princes and nobles in northern Germany. One of the appeals of Protestantism was religious independence from the church in Rome and the loosening of the bonds that tied them to the Holy Roman Empire. Eventually, as more and more princes joined the Reformation, a period of conflict pitted the Catholic emperor and his supporting nobles against the Protestant princes. After decades of turmoil, the Holy Roman Emperor Karl V called the Reichstag for a meeting at Augsburg, Germany, in 1555. The result of the meeting, the so-called Peace of Augsburg, decreed that ruling princes could determine which of the two recognized religions—Catholicism or Lutheranism—was the official faith of their principality. (Ironically, this ruling contradicted a basic tenet of Lutheranism—that salvation was a personal matter between an individual and God, and could not be constrained by religious or secular rulers.)

THE AUGSBURG CONFESSION is the name given to the Lutheran statement of faith. Its principal author was Philipp Melanchthon, Martin Luther's closest friend and comrade. Melanchthon wanted to create a statement that would not be labeled as a heresy by Catholics in the Holy Roman Empire. Despite his efforts, Catholic leaders did not approve of several parts of the confession, including the rejection of celibacy among the clergy, mandatory confession, and the authority of bishops. Although it did not succeed in placating the Catholic opposition, the Augsburg Confession served as a model for later Protestant sects, including the Anglicans and Methodists in England.

The Augsburg compromise did little to clear up the confusion. For example, Weil der Stadt, Kepler's birth city, was predominantly Catholic. Yet it was situated in the duchy of Württemberg, which was Protestant, as was its ruler, the duke of Württemberg. To protect Weil der Stadt, it was made an imperial city. Its only allegiance was to the Holy Roman Empire, although it was located hundreds of miles from the imperial city of Vienna.

Graz, the capital of Styria and a predominantly Protestant city in a Protestant majority duchy, was another example of the problems created by the Peace of Augsburg. The nobles and middle class in Styria were mostly Protestant, but they were poorly organized and riddled with internal conflicts. After 1555, Styria was ruled by Archduke Charles, a Catholic member of the Hapsburg family. Although Charles had agreed to let the Protestants alone, he died before Kepler arrived, and his widow, Archduchess Maria, a devout Catholic, agitated for the eradication of "Protestant heresy." As Kepler entered Graz, plans were being laid for Maria's son Ferdinand to become the new archduke. Ferdinand, who would cast a long shadow over Kepler's life, had been raised by his mother to carry on the fight to restore Catholic hegemony, or domination, in Europe.

The movement within the Catholic Church to stop the spread of Protestantism is now referred to as the Counter-Reformation. Within the Counter-Reformation was a new religious order called the Society of Jesus, or the Jesuits, which was committed to using education to

After finishing his studies, Kepler moved to Graz and became a teacher of mathematics at a seminary. *(Courtesy of the New York Public Library.)*

maintain the faith. The Jesuits developed a strict educational method that emphasized the classics, rhetoric, and religion. Soon after the Peace of Augsburg, the Jesuits established a school in Graz.

In opposition to the Jesuit educational offensive, Protestants created Stiftsschule, or Stift Seminary, in July 1574. Most of the students were the sons of noblemen and burghers (middle-class town dwellers.) The school was divided into two sections. The lower school for younger students consisted of three groups of ten students. The upper school had four classes and its teachers were called professors. Upper school students were split into three categories, depending on their areas of study: theology, law and history, and philosophy (including logic, metaphysics, rhetoric, classics, and mathematics).

Kepler was hired to teach philosophy in the upper school. He was paid 150 gulden a year, which was barely adequate to cover his expenses. The low salary was not only due to his youth and inexperience, it also reflected the disregard for mathematics at the time. While arithmetic was respected for its practical applications, higher mathematics was considered to be an elaborate system of puzzles with little practical use. One reason that historians refer to Copernicus, Kepler, Galileo Galilei, and others as the first modern scientists is because they consistently used mathematics in their scientific explorations. Kepler had so few mathematics students his first year that his duties were expanded to include classes in rhetoric and classics.

Kepler got along well with the first headmaster, who was called to teach at Tübingen soon after his arrival. He was not as fortunate with the successor, who felt the young professor did not show him enough respect. Kepler was not a great teacher. He talked so rapidly the boys had difficulty following him, and his lectures tended to stray off subject. Despite these deficiencies, most of his superiors approved of Kepler and gave him good evaluations.

In addition to teaching, Kepler was the district mathematician and calendar maker. In 1595, he created his first calendar—five more would follow—complete with astrological predictions for the coming year. Astrology was a popular pursuit in the Renaissance, and while Kepler believed that heavenly bodies did influence people and events, he also thought most astrological predictions were intended to sway important people. He thought a more accurate astrology, based on science, could be developed.

Kepler wrote about astrology and other aspects of his intellectual development during his first, lonely months in Graz. As usual in his autobiographical writings, he referred to himself in the third person:

[Kepler] was born destined to spend much time on difficult tasks from which others shrunk. He loved mathematics above all other studies . . . and explored various fields of mathematics as if he were the first man to do so . . . He argued with men of every profession for the profit of his mind. He tended to be highly critical of himself, citing his inconsistency, thoughtlessness, lack of discipline and rashness . . . lack of persistence in his undertakings, caused by the quickness of his spirit . . . beginning many new tasks before the previous one is finished . . . sudden enthusiasms which do not last, for, however industrious he may be, nevertheless he is a bitter hater of work.

Kepler longed for home during his first months in Graz. He even wrote to Maestlin in hopes of arranging a job back in Germany. Painfully aware of his inadequacies as a teacher, he was still uncertain he had made the right decision to not enter the clergy. While occasionally overly enthusiastic during intellectual discussions, he did manage to impress his colleagues with his generous spirit as well as with his intelligence.

It was during these first long months that he first turned his attention to philosophy and astronomy in a systematic manner. He had studied the subjects as a student, but now, freed from his theological studies, he began to speculate on the astronomical ideas he had found so fascinating at Tübingen.

Kepler questioned things others took for granted. What was the world made of? Why were there six planets? (At the time, only Mercury, Venus, Earth, Mars, Jupiter, and Saturn were known.) Why were they placed where they were? What determined the distances between the planetary orbits? Why did the planets seem to move more slowly when farthest from the Sun?

Twenty-first century scientists realize that asking the simplest question has the potential to reveal an entirely new way of understanding nature, but in the seventeenth century it was an unusual method. For an academic of Kepler's time to question Aristotle was to risk embarrassment. Did he not understand the Aristotelian system? The idea that taking another look at the basic assumptions of astronomy could be beneficial, even necessary, did not occur to the vast majority of philosophers. Kepler also thought about nature in terms of mass, size, and quantity.

Pythagoras wrote the world was designed mathematically and the human mind was designed to understand nature in terms of quantity and mass. Kepler agreed with this assertion. The more we think in numbers, Kepler wrote, the clearer our thinking becomes. And conversely, the further we stray from numbers, the more confused we become. To Kepler, the mind of God was mathematics.

One question began to occupy his thoughts more than others: What determined the distance between the planetary intervals? It was not enough to know the size of the orbital intervals. He wanted to know why the orbits were a certain size. When the universe was measured and quantified, what would the measurements mean? Space had to be structured according to a design.

Kepler began to use most of his time out of the classroom pondering these questions, reading, and making calculations. At first, he sought a numerical relationship and worked on the problem, calculation after calculation, for months, without finding a satisfying answer. Then, one day in July 1595, as he stood before his students delivering a lecture and drawing a figure on the chalkboard, he had a revelation. "What I could not obtain with all my efforts was given to me through chance," he wrote in the preface of his first book, *Cosmological Mystery.*

The figure he drew on the board that day was an equilateral triangle contained within a circle. The revelation came when he had a random idea (something his students had come to expect): What if another circle were drawn within the triangle?

He realized that the ratio of the larger circle to the smaller circle was the same as that of the ratio of the orbits of Saturn to Jupiter, the outer of the six known planets. Had he discovered that geometric figures determined the space between the orbits? He began to plug in other shapes—squares, pentagons—in the known intervals of the other planets, looking for a pattern. When this failed to produce the desired results, he had another insight: Space was three dimensional, so why be limited by two-dimensional shapes?

Everything then seemed to fall into place. There are

KEPLER AND THE PLATONIC SOLIDS

The Platonic, or perfect, solids are three-dimensional figures with sides that are identical in shape and size. There are only five platonic solids:

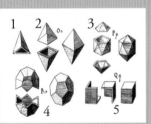

1) tetrahedron: four triangular sides
2) octahedron: eight triangular sides
3) icosahedron: twenty triangular sides
4) dodecahedron: twelve pentagonal sides
5) cube: six square sides

One aspect of the solids that intrigued Kepler was that each could be inscribed in and circumscribed around a sphere. Later, while writing *World Harmony*, in which he sought to define the unity of all natural phenomena, Kepler associated each of the five solids with one of the classic elements: tetrahedron to fire, cube to earth, octahedron to air, icosahedron to water, and the dodecahedron to aether, the immutable substance that existed beyond the sublunary region.

only five possible three-dimensional forms, the so-called "Platonic" solids. In Kepler's mind, a pattern emerged—six planets, five intervals between the planets, five perfect solids. Perhaps the solids represented the mathematical relationship between the planets that Kepler had been searching for.

With this new model, Kepler was convinced he was looking into God's mind. He later wrote that the breakthrough caused him to burst into tears. "I believe it was by divine ordinance that I obtained by chance that which previously I could not reach by any pains." He began work immediately on a book explaining his discovery. He laid out the thesis in one sentence: "The earth is the measure for all other orbits."

Kepler worked on the book over the summer and fall of 1595 and into the next year. In February 1596, he finished his first draft before returning to Germany to visit his aging grandfather and to talk over his theories with Maestlin.

While in Germany, Kepler visited the court of the duke of Württemberg. He told the duke about his discovery and his plans to publish it in a book. When Maestlin assured the duke that Kepler's ideas were worthwhile, the duke asked Kepler to build him a model of his geometrical design in copper. Kepler agreed and designed a paper model, but after two years of planning, the copper model was never completed.

Kepler returned to Graz in August. He had been granted a leave of only two months, but he had stayed

Prodromus

DISSERTATIONVM COSMOGRA-
PHICARVM, CONTINENS MYSTE-
RIVM COSMOGRAPHI-
CVM,

DE ADMIRABILI
PROPORTIONE ORBIVM
COELESTIVM, DEQVE CAVSIS
coelorum numeri, magnitudinis, motuumque pe-
riodicorum genuinis & pro-
prijs,
DEMONSTRATVM, PER QVINQVE
regularia corpora Geometrica,

A

CM. IOANNE KEPLERO, VVIRTEM-
bergico, Illustrium Styriæ prouincia-
lium Mathematico.

Quotidiè morior, fateorque: sed inter Olympi
Dum tenet assiduas me mea cura vias:
Non pedibus terram contingo: sed ante Tonantem
Nectare, diuina pascor & ambrosiâ.

Addita est erudita NARRATIO M. GEORGII IOACHIMI
RHETICI, de Libris Reuolutionum, atque admirandis de numero, or-
dine, & distantijs Sphærarum Mundi hypothesibus, excellentissimi Ma-
thematici, totiusque Astronomiæ Restauratoris D. NICOLAI
COPERNICI.

⋙ ⋘
✦

TVBINGÆ
Excudebat Georgius Gruppenbachius,
ANNO M. D. XCVI.

Kepler's first book, *Cosmological Mystery*, explored his ideas regarding the structure of the universe. *(Courtesy of the Houghton Library, Harvard University. From* Cosmological Mystery, *1596.)*

away almost seven. His superiors at the school forgave him. They had come to appreciate Kepler's mind and hoped that his book would bring honor to the school. In the spring of 1597, twenty-five-year-old Johannes Kepler held in his hands a copy of his first book, *Cosmological Mystery* or *The Secret of the Universe*. The tiny book sold for only ten kreuzers, less than a nickel. Kepler had to purchase and distribute two hundred copies himself as part of the arrangement with the printer. He sent copies to major scholars and practicing astronomers, including Tycho Brahe in Denmark and Galileo Galilei in Italy.

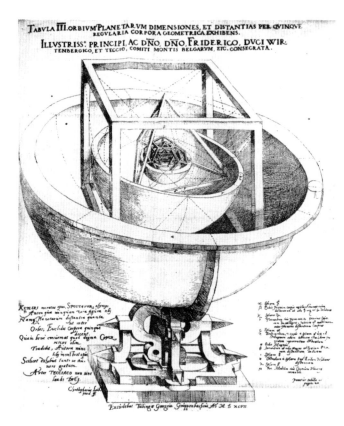

Kepler developed a model of the universe based on the five Platonic solids. *(Courtesy of the Houghton Library, Harvard University. From* Cosmological Mystery, *1596.)*

Cosmological Mystery was the first published astronomical work that accepted Copernican theory. After receiving his copy, Galileo wrote back that he also was convinced of heliocentrism and a moving Earth but was not ready to publicly express his support. When Kepler responded by asking him to speak out, Galileo dropped the correspondence. It would be several years before Galileo announced his support of Copernicus's system.

While Kepler's geometrical theory of planetary organization was erroneous, its conceptualization, and the book based on it, marked the beginning of his journey toward his great discoveries. It also showed an independence of mind that would serve him well. Although a committed Copernican, Kepler was not afraid to disagree with Copernicus when necessary. Most critically, at this early date, he rejected Copernicus's use of additional epicycles. Kepler was also convinced the Sun provided the force that moved the planets, and that the force was proportional to a planet's distance from the Sun. Orbital period (the time it took a planet to complete its orbit) was not only a result of the distance a planet traveled, as Copernicus had said, but it was also dependent on its distance from the Sun.

Kepler was not entirely happy with *Cosmological Mystery*. He knew he had not proven his theory of Platonic solids. One problem was that he needed better information on planetary orbits. The Danish astronomer Tycho Brahe was the only person in the world who had this information.

Kepler's methodology in *Cosmological Mystery* consisted of wild flights of imagination, brilliant insights, and mathematical analysis. It was the work of an emerging scientist. Even later, when he was well aware of its deficiencies, he always expressed affection for the book and saw it as the basis of his life's search for celestial harmony.

By the time Kepler finished *Cosmological Mystery*, he had determined there was no conflict between religion and scientific reasoning. Both were part of one great plan. He wanted to publish an introduction to

Cosmological Mystery that argued the Copernican theory was more consistent with God's plan than the geocentric model, but his friend Matthias Hafenreffer, a prominent Protestant, convinced him that it would cause major divisions among scholars, as well as between scholars and theologians. The ensuing scandal would distract from the real message of the work. A few decades in the future, Galileo would disregard similar advice and consequently be tried for heresy.

After its publication, response from scientists ranged from enthusiasm, to bafflement, to disagreement. The principal complaint was that he mixed theoretical physics with astronomy. Astronomy was supposed to be a practical craft used to make calendars and astrological charts and to navigate the seas. The idea of combining astronomy with speculation about geometrical shapes and numerical ratios, not to mention discussing the physical causes of planetary motion, offended the sensibilities of many teachers.

Most importantly to the future of astronomy, Tycho Brahe responded positively to the book in a letter to Kepler. Although Tycho rejected Copernicus's heliocentricism and advocated his own geocentric model of the universe, he admired Kepler's systematic approach and recognized an original mind. He finished his letter by inviting Kepler to visit him at his new home in Prague.

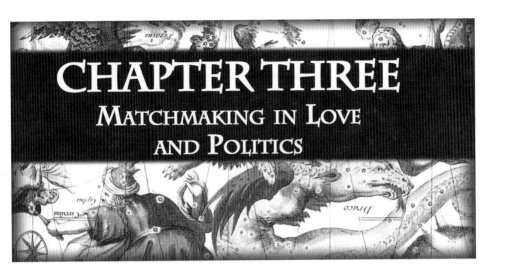

CHAPTER THREE
MATCHMAKING IN LOVE AND POLITICS

During the months spent writing *Cosmological Mystery*, Kepler did not devote all of his time to work. He was also busy planning his wedding. He had met Barbara Mueller, the pretty, plump, oldest daughter of a mill owner named Jobst Mueller in December 1595. Barbara, who lived two hours south of Graz, was only twenty-three, but had already been twice widowed. She had first been married at sixteen to a wealthy, much older cabinetmaker, with whom she had a daughter. After two years, he died. The second marriage was to another elderly man who came to the marriage in ill health and died soon after. Both marriages had been arranged by her father, who was a wealthy and ambitious landowner.

In January 1596, Kepler decided to try to arrange a marriage with Barbara. He sent two representatives to her father to recommend him and to make his intentions known. Although Jobst Mueller was not overjoyed with the prospect of Kepler as a prospective son-in-law because of his low pay and uncertain future, he finally agreed. Unfortunately, soon afterwards, Kepler left for home in Germany to visit his ailing grandfather. When he returned nearly seven months later, Barbara was no longer available, as her father had decided to find a wealthier match. Kepler, though, refused to accept defeat, and when Mueller's search for a husband failed to produce a replacement, the betrothal of Johannes Kepler and Barbara Mueller was announced. The couple was married on April 27, 1597.

Early on, the marriage was happy. Kepler deeply loved his stepdaughter, Regina, and enjoyed domestic life, although he worried constantly about money. He soon learned, however, that his family could often be a source of grief, as well as contentment. Nine months after the wedding, a son named Heinrich was born, but he died sixty days later. In June 1599, the couple had a daughter they named Susanna. She lived for only thirty-five days.

Under this pressure, Kepler's marital happiness did not last. Losing children, although not uncommon in this era, depressed both Johannes and Barbara. There were other problems, too. Barbara had little intellectual curiosity and even less interest in her husband's work. She

Kepler married his first wife, Barbara, in 1597. *(Courtesy of the Museum of the Russian Academy of Sciences, St. Petersburg.)*

only read her prayer book and resented Johannes's meager salary and the unsettled life of a professor. After a few months of marriage, he referred to Barbara in a letter to Maestlin as "simple of mind and fat of body" and "confused and perplexed." Years later, he recalled that although she lavished love on her children, "not much love came my way." He also admitted that some of the tension was because "I never called her a fool, though it may have been her understanding that I considered her a fool, for she was very touchy."

Kepler's marriage was not the only deteriorating situation in his life in the years 1597 and 1598. A few months before his wedding, eighteen-year-old Archduke Ferdinand became the ruler of Inner Austria, which included Styria. Soon after assuming office, Ferdinand set about attempting to restore Catholic supremacy. In the spring of 1597, Ferdinand traveled to Rome to meet with the pope to discuss how best to proceed with the Counter-Reformation. While he was gone, all of Graz was filled with rumors of what would happen when he returned. The most ominous prediction was that the young archduke would bring with him a legion of the pope's soldiers. "Everything trembles in anticipation of the return of the prince," Kepler wrote to Maestlin.

Several prominent citizens reacted to Ferdinand's trip to Rome by advocating a preemptive revolt. Some of the more radical ministers made crude comments and drawings about the Virgin Mary and attacked the arch-duke and the pope from the pulpit. These actions played into Ferdinand's hands. Soon after his return in June 1598, he issued a proclamation denying all non-Catho-lics "every exercise of religion, the administering of the sacrament and the consecration of marriages." He said the edicts were necessary to protect his Catholic sub-jects. When Protestant leaders protested the move, he had them arrested as threats to public safety. On Septem-ber 23, all clergy and teachers were ordered to either convert to Catholicism or leave Graz within eight days, upon penalty of death.

On September 28, Ferdinand issued an even more stringent order: All Protestant preachers, rectors, and school employees had to leave Graz by sundown that day, or face arrest and possible execution. Needless to say, all departed, including Kepler, who left his wife and family behind. In October, Kepler was permitted to return to Graz, the only Protestant teacher allowed to do so. No public reason for this exemption was given. He did have several friends among the Jesuits, who respected his mathematical expertise and may have intervened on his behalf.

Kepler was treated better than his fellow teachers, but Ferdinand's actions created havoc in the newly married professor's life. Although a Protestant like her husband, the decrees applied only to professionals, and Barbara insisted on staying in Styria when Kepler had to leave. When his second child died, he was fined ten dalers for attempting to bury him with the Lutheran burial rites. Half the fine was eliminated after he appealed, but the other half had to be paid before burial.

Kepler's time in Graz was coming to an end. In August 1599, he wrote Maestlin requesting help in finding a job. Maestlin waited five months before answering: "If only you had sought the advice of men wiser and more experienced in politics than I, who am, I confess, as inexperienced in such matters as a child."

The school was closed down, although Kepler continued to receive his salary. He took advantage of his forced idleness to contemplate what he wanted to study next. Still intrigued by the deeper aspects of planetary harmony, he was convinced that the universe was interdependent. Kepler surmised the Sun provided the causal force and this force must operate on all the planets in the same way. But how powerful was this force, and how much did it vary over distance? To determine this, he would have to study a single planet and determine how its speed fluctuated relative to its position.

Kepler also took a look at his own inadequacies. His eyesight was too poor to make his own observations. His personality was not suited for making steady, consistent observations and measurements. He also believed his knowledge of mathematics was still inadequate.

There was one man in Europe who could solve most of his problems: Tycho Brahe. The Dane could probably arrange for his new patron, Emperor Rudolph II in Prague, to give Kepler a job, or maybe Tycho could pay Kepler himself. Tycho was a wealthy man in his own right who, prior to moving to Prague, had spent twenty years collecting the most extensive and accurate naked-eye

Danish astronomer Tycho Brahe hired Kepler as one of his assistants. *(Courtesy of The Royal Library, Copenhagen.)*

observations ever assembled. Tycho had recently left Denmark after a dispute with the country's new king. Tycho had also invited Kepler to visit him in his new home near Prague.

There was a definite downside to aligning himself too closely to Brahe, a famously garrulous man who had a reputation for secrecy. Kepler would need to tap yet unseen resources of tact if he were to, "wrest his [Brahe's] riches from him," as he wrote. He could spend years in Tycho's service and never be allowed to use the observations for his own purposes. However, as his situation in Graz worsened, he decided it was a chance he was willing to take.

Tycho Brahe had studied throughout Germany and Austria until he was twenty-six. As a young student making his first observations, he discovered that the planetary tables then in use were not very accurate. The oldest son of a prominent Danish noble family, he had resisted his family's pressure to take on a career in law or diplomatic service and dedicated his life to measuring the heavens. Although these measurements were taken using the best instruments available, Tycho's observations were made with the "naked eye." The use of the telescope in astronomy was not introduced until 1609. His patron, King Frederick II of Denmark, had funded the building of a massive astronomical research facility on the island of Hven in the sound east of Copenhagen. Tycho spent a great deal of the king's money to build Uraniborg, the world's most elaborate

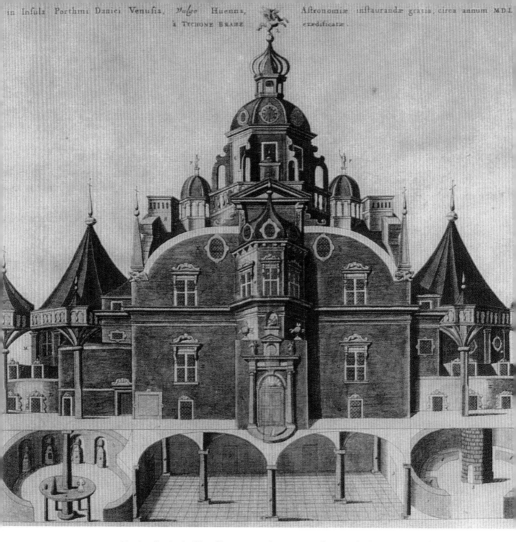

Tycho Brahe's Uraniborg was the most advanced observatory of its time.
(Courtesy of The Royal Library, Copenhagen.)

observatory. Word of Tycho's island, with its huge instruments, planetarium, underground bunkers, and running
water, spread throughout Europe.

Tycho Brahe ran Uraniborg like a modern research
institute. He and his assistants designed and built instruments, made measurements, and developed star catalogs. Tycho also wrote several books, including works
on the new star of 1572 and the comet of 1577. Tycho's

time at Hven ended when he was fifty-one. At that time, a new young Danish king, Christian IV, who disapproved of Tycho's often tyrannical administration of the island and his drain on the public purse, came to power. An angry Tycho left his native country, never to return, and searched for a new patron. Ultimately, and fortunately for the future of astronomy, he ended up in Prague, where he was granted the job of imperial mathematician at the court of Emperor Rudolph II, with a salary of three thousand florins per year, fifteen times what Kepler was paid as a professor.

Kepler and Brahe were brought together by mutual need. Kepler needed Brahe's observations, instruments, and a salary; Brahe needed Kepler's theoretical genius to put his life's work to use. Their relationship, however, was complicated. Tycho was opposed to heliocentricism on religious and physical grounds. He had developed his own theory of the universe, in which the planets orbit both Earth and the Sun, but Earth remains stationary. He also felt old age coming on and desperately wanted someone to carry on with his theory after his death. Kepler, on the other hand, rejected Tycho's system. There is no evidence he ever considered it seriously; his commitment to heliocentricism never wavered. However, his need for Tycho's measurements, and a steady salary, was more important to him than arguing about Tycho's model of the universe.

In late 1599, Kepler knew it was time to leave Graz. The crackdown on Protestant worship had grown worse.

Emperor Rudolph became Tycho Brahe's patron after the astronomer moved to Prague. *(Courtesy of The Royal Library, Copenhagen.)*

After the preachers had been removed from their positions and the churches closed, worshippers began to go to the estates of Protestant noblemen for services and to receive the sacraments. When the Catholic hierarchy realized what was happening, they outlawed visits to the estates and began to force families to baptize their children as Catholics. The newly baptized children could only attend Catholic schools and were expected to marry Catholics as adults. Anyone caught singing Protestant hymns or reading the Lutheran Bible could be banished from Styria. All books were checked for heretical passages.

In January 1600, at the age of twenty-eight, Kepler learned that a friendly local Catholic official and amateur scientist, Baron Johann Friedrich Hoffmann, a councilor to Holy Roman Emperor Rudolph II, was going to Prague. The baron offered to take Kepler along and to present him to his friend Tycho Brahe. Kepler had little choice but to leave his family behind and make the trip. In the meantime, Brahe, having heard of Kepler's desperate situation and eager to have him as an assistant, wrote him another encouraging letter inviting him to visit. Kepler never read the letter—he had left Graz with Baron Hoffmann before it arrived.

CHAPTER FOUR
TYCHO'S SHADOW

When Brahe heard that Kepler had arrived in Prague in January 1600, he dashed off a welcoming letter from his home outside the city. "You will come not so much as a guest, but as a very welcome friend and highly desirable participant and companion in our observation of the heavens."

That Tycho was eager for Kepler to visit is an indication of how much he thought he needed him. Even more surprising, Brahe's welcoming letter came after an embarrassing episode a few years earlier that could have destroyed the relationship before it began. In November 1595, Kepler wrote a letter of lavish praise to Raimarus Ursus, who was then serving as Emperor Rudolph's mathematician. Kepler did not know when he wrote the letter that Ursus and Tycho were in the middle of an ugly dispute. Ursus charged that the Dane had stolen his planetary model. Tycho, in turn, insisted that Ursus had stolen the idea from him during a visit to his observatory in Denmark. Ursus wrote a book attacking Tycho that was so mean-spirited it resulted in his dismissal as imperial mathematician. Kepler became embroiled in the conflict when Ursus, without asking his permission, printed Kepler's flattering letter in his book.

When he first wrote to Tycho, Kepler was unaware of the conflict and that Ursus had printed his letter in his book. Ironically, Tycho received his first copy of Ursus's book on the same day he received Kepler's letter. When he became aware of the situation, Kepler wrote Tycho a letter of apology and made it clear he supported him in the conflict. Tycho accepted the apology, but later asked Kepler to write a pamphlet denouncing Ursus.

In February 1600, Kepler visited Benátky, Brahe's estate, for the first time. At their first meeting, fifty-three-year-old Brahe was tired and homesick, although still mentally and physically active. Kepler, twenty-eight, stood at the beginning of his career. The two men were different in other ways. The nobleman was self-assured to the point of arrogance; Kepler lacked Tycho's bravado. Brahe thrived among groups of people and was usually surrounded by family, friends, and assistants, even during meals. Kepler relished solitude and was happiest in his study.

Kepler had hoped he would be assigned the task of mapping the orbit of Mars, but Longomontanus, another of Tycho Brahe's assistants, was given the project. *(Courtesy of The Royal Library, Copenhagen.)*

Benátky was located twenty-two miles northeast of Prague, about a six-hour ride from the city. Brahe, who had moved to the castle six months earlier, sent his son and namesake, Tyge, and his future son-in-law, Franz Tengnagel, in a carriage to the city to pick up Kepler.

Upon his arrival at Benátky, Kepler and Brahe exchanged pleasantries before entering into negotiations. Kepler listed his requirements: A separate apartment, regular salary from the emperor, provisions for firewood and meat, fish, beer, bread, and wine, a request for input on how he should spend his time and on what, and the right to rest during the day if he worked late at night. Brahe explained he had gotten no word from the emperor yet regarding salary, but he wanted Kepler to remain until news arrived. This did not satisfy Kepler, who flew into a rage and left immediately for Prague. In the city, he wrote an angry note to Brahe. Within the week, however, he followed his note with an apology. Three weeks later, Brahe traveled to Prague and brought Kepler back with him to Benátky.

During his months in Tycho's employ, Kepler often found himself in competition with two of Tycho's other assistants. Tengnagel was engaged to one of Brahe's daughters. Christian Sorensen, known by his Latin name Longomontanus, had worked with Tycho at Uraniborg for over a decade and was close to the Brahe family. Kepler felt that Longomontanus received the best assignments. While Longomontanus was allowed to work on plotting the orbit of Mars, for example, Kepler had to work on the pamphlet refuting Ursus's claims. This was particularly galling because Kepler had come to think that Mars and its eccentric orbit held the key to unlocking the mystery of planetary motion.

Kepler was anxious to begin work on plotting the orbit of Mars, but Tycho was not interested in developing new theories. He wanted to finish work on a set of new planetary tables he had promised the emperor and his other projects as well. Kepler also despaired of ever receiving the data necessary to test his theory of the five solids and wondered if he had made a mistake throwing his lot in with Tycho. But there was nowhere else to turn. As he wrote to Maestlin:

> Tycho possesses the best observations and . . . lacks

only the architect who uses all this according to a plan ... He is hindered by the diversity of the phenomena as well as by the fact that the truth lies hidden extremely deep within them. Now old age steals upon him, weakening his intellect and other faculties, or, after a few years, will so weaken them that it will be difficult for him to accomplish everything alone.

In June 1600, Kepler had to return to Styria to take care of his wife's estate. Emperor Rudolph had failed to give him a salary yet, and he carried a letter of recommendation from Brahe to the Styrian councilors asking that they continue his professor's salary while he worked with Brahe in Prague. He continued to hope that he would be able to return to his teaching position at some point. He also sent a long letter to Archduke Ferdinand outlining his astronomical ideas and asking for a position as mathematician. Despite the religious differences, Ferdinand had always been gracious toward Kepler. There was a chance he could stay on the archduke's payroll.

Archduke Ferdinand ignored Kepler's request. Instead, in July, he published a decree ordering all of his subjects to appear before specified tribunals in five days so that authorities could determine whether they had the "correct" faith. All non-Catholics would be banished. Kepler appeared as ordered, refused conversion to Catholicism, and was ordered to leave. Although he was given a letter of recommendation and half a year's salary, he was no longer welcome in Graz. When Kepler told Brahe of this new development, Tycho encouraged him to return to Prague, where he promised to work out a salary arrangement with Emperor Rudolph.

Brahe was motivated to find Kepler a salary in part because Longomontanus had returned to Denmark along with many of his other assistants. For his part, Kepler had little choice but to return to Prague. In September 1600, he left Graz with his wife, stepdaughter, and two wagons of household goods. En route, he became ill with a persistent fever, which slowed his progress. In October, a tired and dejected Kepler arrived in Prague. By now, the fever was accompanied by a bad cough, and his wife was also ill.

When he was well enough to begin work again, Kepler was still faced with the task of finishing the pamphlet attacking Ursus. This chore took time away from astronomical studies. In the spring of 1601, Kepler was allowed to return to Graz when his wife's father died. He was away from Prague from the end of April until the beginning of September. During that time, Kepler's wife wrote him that Brahe had not given her the allowance that he had promised. After Kepler complained angrily, the two eventually reached an agreement, but hard feelings remained.

Kepler returned to Prague in the autumn of 1601, healthy and refreshed. Brahe introduced him to the emperor, and their interview went smoothly. It was a fortunate meeting. A few weeks later, Tycho Brahe became ill after a party. He died on October 24, 1601. Kepler was at his deathbed during his last days. Before he died, Brahe begged Kepler to carry on his work.

Tycho Brahe was buried November 4, 1601, amid much pomp and ceremony. Two days after the funeral, an imperial advisor came with news that the emperor was transferring to Kepler the care of Tycho's instruments and research. He appointed Kepler the new imperial mathematician and requested he begin work completing the new astronomical tables that Tycho had started. Tycho had asked that he be allowed to call the completed work the *Rudolphine Tables*, in honor of Emperor Rudolph, and permission was granted.

A few months after Kepler's appointment, Tengnagel returned to Prague to protest the emperor's decision. Tengnagel had some claim to Brahe's legacy as he had married Tycho's daughter and she had given birth to their child. They had since moved back to Denmark. A promise had been made to pay Tycho's heirs for the instruments and the papers, but no payment had been forthcoming. Tengnagel insisted he also be given a job. Rudolph commissioned him to work on the *Rudolphine Tables*.

Tengnagel's new job threatened Kepler. To secure his position, Kepler wrote to Emperor Rudolph in October 1602 and promised to complete two books by the next spring. One book would concern optical astronomy, and the other a study of Mars. In reality, the book on optics would not be ready for two years, and the Mars book was

Kepler published a book on optics that explained how the human eye processes light. *(From Johannes Kepler, Optical Part of Astronomy.)*

AD VITELLIONEM
PARALIPOMENA,
Quibus
ASTRONOMIÆ
PARS OPTICA
TRADITVR;
Potissimum
DE ARTIFICIOSA OBSERVATIO-
NE ET ÆSTIMATIONE DIAMETRORVM
deliquiorumq; Solis & Lunæ.
CVM EXEMPLIS INSIGNIVM ECLIPSIVM.
Habes hoc libro, Lector, inter alia multa noua,
*Tractatum luculentum de modo visionis , & humorum oculi
vsu,contra Opticos & Anatomicos,*
AVTHORE
IOANNE KEPLERO, S. C. Mᵗⁱ
Mathematico.

FRANCOFVRTI,
Apud Claudium Marnium & Hæredes Ioannis Aubrii
Anno M. DCIV.
Cum Privilegio S. C. Maiestatis.

not published until 1609. The ploy succeeded, however. Kepler firmly seated himself as imperial mathematician.

The work on optics, which was published as *Optical Part of Astronomy,* began as a study of solar eclipses. Before his death, Tycho attempted to measure a solar eclipse by making a pinhole-sized aperture, or opening, and reflecting the eclipse on a screen. Tycho measured the image and determined that a total eclipse was impossible. Kepler, however, refused to accept this conclusion, conducted his own experiments on a partial eclipse in 1601, and wrote an essay arguing that Tycho's measurements were wrong because of the size of the aperture. He decided to expand his work into a book and analyze how the eye sees light, among other topics.

Optical Part of Astronomy is divided into two sections. The part on pure optics begins with a discussion of the nature of light. Kepler proposed light spreads out from a point, and its intensity decreases the farther it travels from its source. He attempted, but failed, to give an accurate account of how light bends, or refracts, but he did make an approximation accurate enough to be used by later researchers.

The most important part of the book deals with the human eye and the process of vision. It was generally believed that light was somehow captured by the eye. Kepler argued that light was not captured by the eye but was refracted on the retina. He also correctly stated that images are re-refracted upside down on the retina and are set upright by a process in the brain he did not attempt to explain. He discussed how both eyes work together to provide depth perception and how eyeglasses improve vision. He discussed various astronomical topics, such as the distances of the Moon, Sun and planets, and the light and shadows of various heavenly bodies.

Optical Part of Astronomy eventually ran to 450 pages. He dedicated it to Emperor Rudolph and presented him the manuscript in April 1604. It was a major step forward in understanding light and how light is perceived by the eye. Not only did the book have significant ramifications for astronomy, it helped to solidify Kepler's hold on the position of imperial mathematician. Although the tension with Tengnagel would continue, for eleven years Kepler drew a steady salary and was able to focus on his work. He devoted much of that time to the study of Mars.

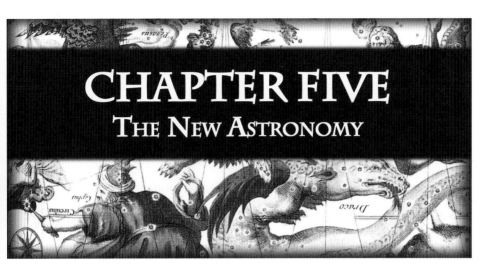

CHAPTER FIVE
THE NEW ASTRONOMY

In *Cosmological Mystery*, Kepler endorsed Copernicus's theory of a stationary Sun and moving Earth. This was a bold step for a young astronomer. What made it even bolder is that he did so despite a lack of physical evidence. His contemporary, Galileo, then a professor of mathematics at the University of Padua near Venice, did not publicly support Copernicus until he had used the recently invented telescope to discover the moons of Jupiter in 1610.

As mentioned earlier, Kepler's unwavering belief in heliocentricism was motivated by a combination of mathematical reasoning and religious mysticism. He was a theology student before he was an astronomer and approached his scientific work with a religious fervor that led him to argue that the Sun was the engine of the universe. This idea was the most controversial aspect of *Cosmological Mystery*. Even his old teacher Maestlin criticized him for it. It was not acceptable, he said, to speculate on physical forces in a book on astronomy. Aristotle had explained the *why* and *how* of planetary motion. Astronomers were supposed to limit themselves to *what*—to making models that could be used to determine where a celestial body would be at a specific time. Astronomy was descriptive only. It was acceptable to suggest new planetary arrangements, as Ptolemy, Copernicus, and Tycho had done, but not to question where the energy that drove the planets originated.

Kepler, characteristically, did not let this criticism deter him. In his mind, now that the Sun had been placed in its rightful place, everything about the universe was open for analysis. He began with the most basic question: Why was the Sun at the hub of the planets? He proposed what seemed to him to be the most obvious answer: To propel the planets along their orbits.

Because Kepler proposed that a planet's speed was determined by its relative distance from the Sun. He knew from his work on optics that light rays weakened over distance, and likewise, he believed the Sun's force weakened in a similar way.

Kepler got his first opportunity to test his theories when, shortly before Tycho's death, the Danish astronomer asked him to take over the long delayed project of mapping the orbit of Mars, one of the most eccentric orbits of all the known planets. (Only Mercury, which was too close to the Sun to be observed consistently, was more eccentric.) Mars was one of the principal reasons Ptolemy introduced the equant into astronomy centuries before.

Kepler decided to try a different strategy than Longomontanus had used to observe Mars. He wanted to know the radius of the orbit, where its speed varied, and by how much. Instead of another mathematical model that could be adjusted to fit the facts, he wanted to use mathematics to describe the physical laws of planetary orbit as they existed.

When he began working, Kepler bragged to Tycho he would be finished with the job in a week. It is easy to imagine Tycho shaking his head, and Kepler soon feeling foolish for making such an impulsive comment. The work was first interrupted by Tycho's death, then by Kepler's work on optics. When he returned to studying Mars in 1601, it became the most exhausting project of his life.

Today, because of Kepler's work, we know that Mars does not travel a circular orbit. Kepler, though, began with the assumption that all orbits were circular and developed his strategies to fit this theory.

Kepler began by dividing the orbit into 360 degrees and measuring the distance from Mars to the Sun at each degree. (Calculus, which is used to measure the rates of change, had not yet been invented.) He hoped to use these raw numbers to determine the radius of the orbit

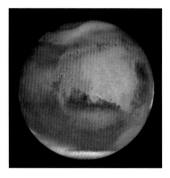

Kepler's measurements of the orbit of Mars helped lead him to the discovery of his three laws of planetary motion. Here, Mars is pictured by the Hubble Space Telecope on June 26, 2001. *(NASA and The Hubble Heritage Team (STScI/AURA).)*

and to arrive at a value for the period (time) it took to move from each degree. Tycho's data was accurate up to two degrees, which meant the sum of the calculations for the entire orbit should not vary more than that. Before Tycho, a ten-degree variance was not uncommon.

Kepler made over nine hundred pages of figures before he finished his calculations. He kept a running record of his work that was later printed in his book, *New Astronomy.* In the middle of this tedious work, he pauses to address the reader, "If this wearisome method has filled you with loathing, it should more properly fill you with compassion for me, as I have gone through it at least seventy times at the expense of a great deal of time, and you will cease to wonder that the fifth year has now gone by since I took up Mars."

Finally, Kepler arrived at a figure that he hoped would be the numerical value of the radius of the orbit. He had reserved two of Tycho's best observations, taken when Mars was in opposition, to check his calculations. When he applied the measurements, he discovered a discrepancy of eight degrees, well outside the acceptable margin of error. "Who would have thought it possible?" he wrote.

OPPOSITION

A planet is in opposition when it is opposite the Sun as seen from Earth. The best time to observe the planets is when they are in opposition, as this is when they are generally closest to Earth. The opposition effect is most easily noticed with Mars.

DIAGRAM

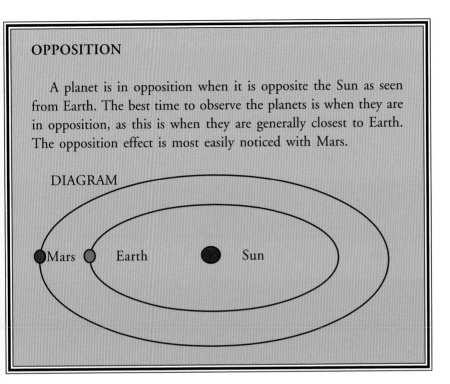

Mars   Earth   Sun

No amount of adjusting made the figures work. It was a disappointing conclusion to years of steady computation, but Kepler was not to be stopped. He approached the problem from a different angle. Maybe he should plot Earth's orbit from the perspective of the Sun. How could he, or any astronomer who believed in a moving Earth, be confident in their measurements until they knew how Earth moved?

When Kepler began his work on Mars, he was still convinced that planets traveled in circular orbits. Although he had once argued with Tycho that the Moon's orbit was not circular, which indicated some early willingness to question the prevalent dogma, he did not begin his work on Mars by questioning the shape of its orbit. His faith in circular orbits was deeply embedded. The circle, which never begins and never ends, was considered a perfect shape. Therefore, in Aristotelian physics, circular motion was the only motion that could possibly exist in the perfect celestial realm. Over the next months, as he continued trying to map Mars, he slowly began to question the notion that planetary orbits were circular.

Kepler began the process of mapping Earth's orbit by following the same procedure he had used on Mars. As he began to work on the calculations, he despaired at having to go through this tedious process again. There had to be another way. What if he divided the orbit into areas and calculated the time it took for the planet to pass through each area? He could, in effect, draw a line from the Sun to the planet and measure the area the line swept out over time. When he attempted this, he made his first great astronomical discovery: A planet's orbit will sweep out over equal areas in equal time intervals. Although he discovered it first, this is now known as Kepler's second law of planetary motion.

The second law geometrically confirms that planets do not move at uniform speeds. Because equal areas are "swept out" in equal time, the farther it is from the Sun, the less distance a planet must travel in the same time interval. (Remember, although he still thought—for a bit longer—that orbits were circular, he did not think the Sun was in the exact center of the orbits.)

The discovery of his second law led directly to the

discovery of what is known as Kepler's first law of planetary motion, but it did not come without another struggle. When he applied the second law to the orbit of Mars, it did not work. There was still an eight minute gap. Because of his faith in his new law, he finally began to

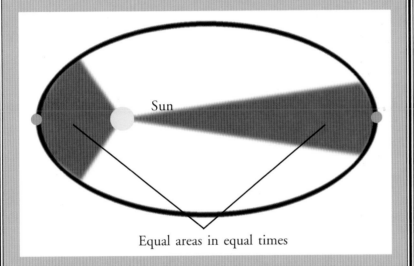

KEPLER'S SECOND LAW OF PLANETARY MOTION

Sun

Equal areas in equal times

To understand Kepler's second law, imagine the planet in this diagram as it moves around the Sun. If you were to draw a straight line from the Sun to the planet, wait one minute, and then draw another line, you would create a pie wedge. Kepler showed that the area of each wedge created at one-minute intervals would be the same, although the wedges would not have the same shape. Nearer the Sun, the wedges will be fatter and cover a larger part of the orbital path; whereas, farther from the Sun, the wedges will be thinner and cover a smaller part of the orbital path.

question circular orbits. He began to imagine different orbital paths to see what shape worked with the law. He first flattened the orbit in the middle. (As he described it, as though he were squeezing a German sausage in the middle, forcing the meat to each end.) But this shape did not fit the measurements.

Kepler decided to use an ellipse to calculate new orbits because the shape was easier to work with, not because he believed orbits were elliptical. An ellipse is a geometrical figure that resembles a slightly flattened circle. Within the ellipse are two imaginary points called the foci, the plural of focus. After several more months of work, he realized that an ellipse fit the measurements better than any other shape. In effect, the answer had been right before him all that time. "I felt as if I had been awakened from a sleep," he wrote about the realization. He had discovered what has come to be called the first law of planetary motion: Planets travel in elliptical orbits, and the Sun is located at one foci.

Kepler had discovered the first two physical laws of the universe. He had used his mind and mathematical skills, combined with Tycho's observational data, to give the human race its first inkling of what actually happened as the planets moved through space. He did not succeed at discovering how the force of the Sun affected the planets. He concluded that it was somehow related to magnetism, and that the Sun pushed the planets along like a spoke on a wheel. It would be left to Isaac Newton to discover that gravitation was a function of attraction, not propulsion.

KEPLER'S FIRST LAW OF PLANETARY MOTION

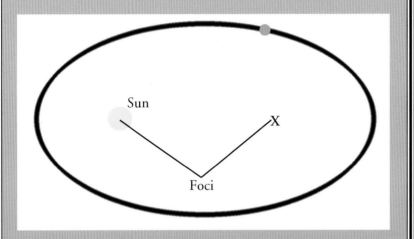

Kepler's first law of planetary motion is represented in the diagram above. The law states that planetary orbits are elliptical, with the Sun positioned at one of two foci. Although Kepler discovered this law second, it is called his first law because elliptical orbits set the foundation for the other two laws.

While Kepler did not make this crowning discovery, he had begun the modern science of physical astronomy by demolishing two thousand years of speculation that had produced circles inside of circles and phantom points in space. He had permanently changed our perspective on the universe by the radical act of letting nature speak for itself.

During the years he did his research and wrote *New Astronomy,* Kepler was often interrupted with the more mundane tasks of his job as imperial mathematician. He had to design and publish calendars with astrological predictions, cast individual horoscopes, write and publish descriptions of eclipses and comets, and maintain official correspondence.

After finally completing the writing of *New Astronomy*, he had to struggle almost as hard to get it published. Tycho's heirs, led by Tengnagel, were opposed to its publication. Their motives were a combination of vanity and greed. Emperor Rudolph had promised to pay the family a huge sum for Tycho's papers. The money had never been paid (it never was), and Tengnagel insisted the observations were still the property of the family. He denied Kepler permission to use them in his work. He was also upset that Kepler had not upheld the Tychonic system.

Tengnagel had a weak spot, however. He dreamed of the completion and publication of the *Rudolphine Tables*, which he was convinced would bring glory and riches to Tycho's heirs. Although he was loath to admit it, he knew that he could not complete the massive project without Kepler's assistance. Kepler shrewdly agreed to help with the tables, but refused to begin work until he published *New Astronomy*. The two men remained at a standstill until they, with the intervention of the emperor, finally reached a compromise: Kepler agreed to let Tengnagel write a preface to the work, in which he warned the reader that Kepler had taken liberties with Brahe's work and legacy.

The next obstacle was money. The emperor granted Kepler four hundred gulden to pay for printing, but the conflict with Tengnagel delayed publication and most of the money went toward living expenses. When printing finally began in 1608, Kepler had to ask for additional money. It was granted but never materialized. When the printer was not paid, Kepler had to give him the entire first edition as payment. He even had to buy copies of his own book to send to other scientists and colleagues.

When it was first published, few of Kepler's contemporaries realized the importance of *New Astronomy*. Those who bothered to write him were polite; a few marveled at his inventiveness. The majority, however, rejected his conclusions. One astronomer wrote, "If you could only preserve the perfect circular orbit, and justify your elliptic orbit by another little epicycle, it would be much better." It would be decades later, when the book made its way to England and into the hands of Isaac Newton, before its revolutionary impact would be appreciated.

CHAPTER SIX
FAME AT THE MERCY OF FATE

Although most of the people who bothered to read it had not grasped the significance of *New Astronomy,* by 1609, Kepler was the most famous astronomer in Europe. (Galileo Galilei had not yet turned his telescope toward Jupiter or entered into his long struggle with the Catholic Church. Most of his time was spent experimenting in physics.) Most remarkably Kepler had succeeded Tycho as the foremost authority on astronomical matters without deviating from his commitment to heliocentricism and a moving Earth. These concepts were still not widely accepted by other scholars.

Kepler's position as imperial mathematician put him in contact with the nobility; counts and barons became godparents to his children. He tried to dress in fine clothes and maintain appearances, but his salary was paid so irregularly he was always deeply in debt.

Prague, as the capital of Bohemia, was at its glorious zenith as a cultural and intellectual center. It was also at the hub of the religious conflict that was simmering to a higher and higher temperature until it boiled over into the Thirty Years' War. Most of the citizens of Bohemia were Protestant, but the ruler, Archduke Rudolph, who was also the Holy Roman Emperor Rudolph II, was Catholic. Under the terms of the Peace of Augsburg, Rudolph could have attempted to impose his religion on the territory he ruled, as Archduke Ferdinand had in Styria. However, during his thirty-six year reign, Rudolph tried to avoid, not press, the issue. Kepler reported the emperor never questioned him about his faith. Rudolph's main interests were art and science. Always a shy man, as Rudolph grew older he became reclusive, sometimes shutting himself off from all human contact for days. He spent most of his time collecting and cataloging his beloved clocks, figurines, gems, fabric, sculpture, carvings, coins, paintings, and other treasures.

This benign neglect may have been the best way to deal with the religious conflict in the past, but tensions grew in the leaderless vacuum. Jesuits and other Catholics established themselves at court in Prague, pushing their goal of reuniting all Christians under the Catholic banner. Rudolph did occasionally bow to the pressure. In 1602, he issued a decree that only Catholics would be tolerated in Bohemia, but he did not follow the decree

After publishing *Cosmological Mystery* and *New Astronomy*, Kepler became the foremost astronomer in Europe. *(Courtesy of the Sternwarte Kremsmünster, Austria.)*

up with action, and conflict was temporarily diverted.

The Protestants in Bohemia had hurt their cause by splintering into several groups. Some maintained a strict Lutheran faith, while others had combined with a group of dissenters that predated the Reformation called the Bohemian Brethren. This group leaned toward the beliefs of John Calvin. Calvinists rejected what they saw as the Catholic influences in the Lutheran creed. They sought to purify Protestantism of all remnants of Catholicism. There was as much tension between these two groups within the Protestant movement as there was between Protestants and Catholics.

Taking advantage of Rudolph's unwillingness to lead, various princes began to take power into their own hands, which led to an increase in armed disputes. In May 1608, the Protestant princes met and agreed to work together. The Catholic leaders soon followed suit. Emperor Rudolph, weary of the issue, began handing over control of various states to his brother Matthias. He gave up control of Austria, Hungary, and Moravia, but attempted to retain control of Bohemia and Silesia. Rudolph issued a royal charter in July 1609 granting the individual princes the power to decide if their provinces would be Protestant or Catholic.

Problems in the Holy Roman Empire extended beyond the religious divisions. Because of Rudolph's neglect, the royal treasury was always near depletion, which meant Kepler's salary often went unpaid. He wrote his friend and patron Herwart von Hohenburg,

"My hungry stomach looks up like a little dog to the master who once fed it." In March 1611, he wrote that the emperor owed him three thousand gulden in back pay. Without the money, he could not afford to hire an assistant to help with computations.

As the situation in Bohemia worsened, Kepler attempted to find a way out. He asked several other princes and nobles for a job, but despite his fame, no one offered him one. It was a stressful time for the most balanced of men; for Kepler it was torture. The tension distracted him from his work. One of the ways it manifested itself was in hypochondria. He wrote to Maestlin:

> You inquire after my illness? It was an insidious fever which originated in the gall and returned four times because I repeatedly sinned in my diet. On May 29 my wife forced me, by her pesterings, to wash, for once, my whole body. She immersed me in a tub (for she has a horror of public baths) with well heated water; its heat afflicted me and constricted my bowels. On May 31, I took a light laxative, according to habit. On June 1, I bled myself, also according to habit: no urgent disease, not even the suspicion of one, compelled me to do it, nor any astrological consideration . . . After losing blood, I felt for a few hours well; but in the evening an evil sleep threw me on my mattress and constricted my guts. Sure enough, the gall at once gained access to my head, bypassing the bowels . . . I think I am one of those people whose gallbladder has a direct opening into the stomach; such people are short lived as a rule.

He had discovered how the planets moved in the heavens but could find no relief from his internal and external stresses. A year after publication of *New Astronomy*, he slipped into a deep depression—"my mind [is] prostrate in a pitiful frost," he wrote.

When he was not filled with despair, Kepler's lively personality and good nature helped him to make friends. He had a keen sense of humor that he loved to turn on himself, a broad knowledge to draw on, and an intriguing intellectual curiosity. He maintained good relationships with both Catholics and Protestants, and the foreign representatives at court enjoyed his company.

In the first years of Kepler's stay in Prague, he spent between four hundred and five hundred gulden annually to maintain his household. As his family grew, he spent between six hundred and one thousand gulden. The family changed residences frequently. From the spring of 1602 to the fall of 1604, they lived opposite the Emaus monastery in New Town. In the fall of 1604, they moved to Wenzel College in Old Town. Beginning in 1607, they lived in the former Cramer buildings opposite the Jesuits by the bridge, where they stayed until leaving Prague.

Barbara gave birth to three children during this decade. In July 1602, she had a daughter Susanna (the first daughter named Susanna had died in 1599, thirty-five days after birth.) Two wives of the imperial guards served as godmothers. In December 1604, their son Friedrich was born. This time, the godfathers were the imperial treasurer, the imperial barrister, and the Baden ambassador. December 1607 brought a son named Ludwig; the godfathers were Count Palatine Philip Ludwig and his son Wofgang Wilhelm von Pfalz-Neuburg.

Kepler's mother visited in 1602, and his sister in 1604. His brother Heinrich was an imperial guard in Prague for eight years, and they saw one another occasionally. In the spring of 1608, Regina, Kepler's step-daughter, married Philip Ehem, representative at the imperial court of Elector Frederick IV of the Palatinate.

Life in the Kepler household did not always run smoothly. In addition to his occasional depressions, he worked obsessively and was prone to flights of fancy, during which he would often try to change all the family's routines. Kepler was not the only source of marital conflict, however. While in public, Barbara was a paragon of charm; at home she was often fiery-tempered. She had been doted on by her father and first two husbands and expected the same treatment from Kepler. She did not understand the importance of his work, nor did she appreciate his talents. Occasionally, people mocked them by referring to the couple as "Mr. and Mrs. Stargazer." He took the jibes with good humor, but she resented them as bitter insults. She worried about money, but spent far too much on the children. Kepler observed that she had "a weak, annoying, solitary, melancholic temperament." He also found her physical and emotional ailments increased with each year. He wrote, "She would have no master and yet often was unable to cope herself."

Kepler usually worked on more than one book at a time. Even while struggling with *New Astronomy*, he wrote a small book about a new star that appeared in 1604. In this work, he argued against using the new star for astrological predictions. After publication of *New Astronomy*, he worked slowly on the *Rudolphine Tables*, while also producing annual books on planetary positions. His other fields of research included the structure of snow flakes, a comet that appeared in September 1607, continued searches for universal harmonies, and the calculation of the birth date of Jesus Christ.

In one work, Kepler carried on a debate with a physician named Helisaeus Roeslin about the validity of astrology. Roeslin defended its use, while Kepler maintained "that the heaven does something in people one sees clearly enough; but what it does specifically remains hidden." He also attempted to connect astrology to his beloved five geometric solids.

In March 1610, Wackher von Wackenfels, a friend and amateur astronomer, rushed to Kepler's house with exciting news. The Italian Galileo Galilei had used a two-lens spyglass to watch the sky and was reporting the discovery of four new planets. Kepler was torn by conflicting emotions. If new planets were discovered, his theory of five solids would no longer be harmonious. At the same time, he found himself filled with "a wonderful emotion while I listened to this curious tale." The excitement of such a discovery was almost overwhelming.

After doing his own research, Kepler decided that

Galileo Galilei announced he had discovered four new planets by use of a telescope. The so-called planets were later proved to be moons of Jupiter. Although Kepler attempted to pursue a professional correspondence with Galileo, the two men never met. *(Courtesy of the National Maritime Museum, London.)*

Galileo had actually observed moons circling Jupiter. That very month, Galileo published a little book, *The Starry Messenger,* and announced the new bodies were indeed satellites and not planets, but that they were all moons of Jupiter. He also claimed that the surface of Earth's moon, like Earth itself, is irregular, with mountains, valleys, and craters.

In April, Kepler received a copy of Galileo's book. The courier waited for Kepler's opinion so he could carry it back to Italy. Kepler spent eleven days composing his thoughts in a letter that was later published with the title *Conversation with the Starry Messenger.*

Kepler's and Galileo's paths first crossed in 1597, when Kepler sent him a copy of *Cosmological Mystery.* Galileo wrote back to thank him for the book, but did not respond to any of Kepler's follow-up letters. Over the next years, Kepler heard a rumor that Galileo had denied ever receiving a copy of *Cosmological Mystery,* although Galileo had been heard teaching Kepler's ideas as his own.

Among scholars, the predominant response to

This photo taken by the Hubble Space Telescope shows four of Jupiter's moons.
(NASA and The Hubble Heritage Team (STScI/AURA).)

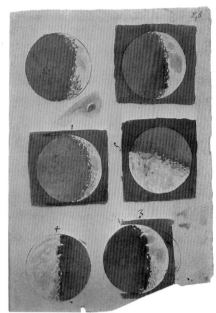

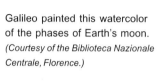

Galileo painted this watercolor of the phases of Earth's moon.
(Courtesy of the Biblioteca Nazionale Centrale, Florence.)

Galileo's book was "doubt, mistrust, challenge, and contradiction." The idea that Jupiter had satellites, when all heavenly bodies were supposed to orbit Earth, and that the Moon's surface was not smooth and crystalline, was shocking. Many simply refused to believe it. Galileo's personality sometimes made the reaction even more negative. He was brilliant but also highly arrogant, rude, and quick to claim credit for discoveries. His enemies sought out any chance to confront him. In addition, when he tried to demonstrate the telescope to skeptics, their lack of experience in using the instrument interfered with sightings, which convinced them that Galileo was playing some sort of trick.

Kepler wanted to find a telescope that he could use to verify Galileo's findings. An influential nobleman asked Galileo to make one available, but the request was ignored, even though Galileo had a workshop that produced them. Kepler, who wanted to support Galileo, asked for names of others who had witnessed his observations, but Galileo did not respond to that request either.

The duke of Bavaria allowed Kepler to borrow his telescope in the summer of 1610. Between August 3 and September 9, the astronomer observed the moons of Jupiter and wrote a pamphlet that confirmed Galileo's discoveries, *Observer's Report on Jupiter's Four Wandering Satellites*. Kepler's support was critical. He went on to write several letters to Galileo—but only one was answered. In his works, Galileo seldom mentioned Kepler, unless it was to refute or minimize his importance. Most critically, to his death, Galileo maintained his belief in circular orbits, epicycles, and deferents. This was despite the fact that Kepler's first two laws were the most convincing evidence of heliocentricism available and could have been helpful in his struggles with the Catholic Church.

Although Galileo never explained to him how the telescope worked, Kepler created a new field, dioptrics—the science of refraction by lenses. In a book entitled *Dioptrice*, written in the same year as *Conversation with the Starry Messenger,* he explained the two-lens system used in telescopes. Galileo made no public comments about *Dioptrice* and did not respond to any more of Kepler's letters. The two men never met.

CHAPTER SEVEN
CHAOS

By 1611, Emperor Rudolph's withdrawal from the world was almost complete. When he was forced to interact with his advisors or foreign visitors, shyness usually paralyzed him. He was unable to reach a decision. All he wanted to do was hide out among his beloved collections.

Ironically, Prague was at the peak of its influence. The emperor's fascination with art helped to generate a thriving business for craftsmen and traders. Ambassadors and other dignitaries held parties and pursued intellectual and cultural activities. Although Kepler shunned the occult and approached his astrological duties as scientifically as possible, the emperor's obsession with astrology and alchemy made the city a center for occultists.

This colorful period in beautiful, cosmopolitan Prague soon drew to a close. As Rudolph continued to ignore his duties, the Hapsburgs met in Vienna and agreed to Matthias's efforts to overthrow Rudolph. Although Rudolph willingly granted Matthias control of Austria, Bavaria, and Hungary, Matthias continued to advance his troops toward Prague. This progress of the more militantly Catholic Matthias frightened the city's Protestant majority. When the Bohemian Estates, an umbrella group of Protestants, pressured Rudolph to guarantee religious freedom, he complied. He then asked his cousin Archduke Leopold of Passau to amass troops at the Bohemian border to help maintain order. Instead, Leopold invaded Bohemia and marched on Prague. Meanwhile, Matthias also entered Prague with his troops. Fighting broke out between soldiers loyal to Leopold and those who fought with Matthias. Matthias forced Rudolph to abdicate (or give up his title) in May 1611. After Leopold left the city, Matthias was crowned king of Bohemia on June 13, 1612.

During all the chaos, Kepler never wavered in his support of Rudolph, even when it might have been to his advantage to shift his loyalty. He continued to create astrological charts for the emperor, but warned against using them to guide military or political strategy.

Kepler's wife, Barbara, became sick at the end of 1610. She suffered from a persistent fever, possibly epilepsy, and mental derangement. In January 1611, three of the Kepler children were stricken with small-pox. His son Frederich, the favorite child, died at age six in February.

After Frederich's death, Barbara became more despondent. She had never liked living in Prague; it was too busy and sophisticated. She felt inadequate with her husband's friends and longed for the quiet life of Graz. Kepler thought returning to Austria would be good for her health and wrote the duke of Württemberg to ask for a position. The duke was inclined to find a way to bring Kepler home, but his clerical advisors were convinced Kepler was a secret Calvinist and refused to recommend him for a position. Galileo had left the University of Padua, near Venice, and Kepler was considered as a possible replacement there, but he was not hired because he was Protestant.

Kepler was not enthusiastic when he was offered a position in Linz, located in Upper Austria. Linz was a "backwater;" there was no university close by, and the job had less prestige than serving as imperial mathematician for the Holy Roman emperor. After the abdication of Rudolph, though, he had little choice. He accepted the post of district mathematician for Upper Austria in June 1611.

Kepler hoped the return to Austria would lighten Barbara's spirits and improve her health. But before they could move, she took ill again with a "Hungarian" fever, probably brought to Prague by Matthias's soldiers. She died on July 3, 1611, at age thirty-seven. They had been married fourteen years. Kepler described her passing:

Stunned by the deeds of horror of the soldiers and the sight of the bloody fighting in the city, consumed by a despair of a better future and by the unquenched yearning for her darling lost son [Frederich], to bring an end to her troubles she was infected by the Hungarian spotted typhus, her mercy taking revenge on her, since she would not be kept away from visiting the sick. In melancholy despondency, the saddest frame of mind under the sun, she finally expired.

The burial service was handled by a notable Lutheran theologian. Kepler had previously written a poem his wife cherished, and he arranged for this to be printed in her memory.

Saddened by his wife's death, and responding to a request from Rudolph, Kepler postponed leaving Prague. He busied himself collecting correspondence from friends and using historical records of eclipses to determine the year of Christ's birth.

After Rudolph died in January 1612, nothing else tied Kepler to Prague. Three months later, he left his children in the temporary care of a widow in Moravia and departed for Linz. He was now forty-one and would remain in Linz for the next fourteen years. His salary at the new position was only four hundred gulden, although payment would be more dependable, and the job was more similar to his earlier one in Graz. He was to be the district mathematician and a teacher in the district school. In addition, he was a much more positive, confident man than he had been when he took his first teaching job. He had written several well-received books and papers and was known by reputation throughout the intellectual circles in Europe. Unfortunately, many in his new home town interpreted his confidence as snobbery. In Graz, he had filled an already available position; in Linz, officials had created a position for him. The school in Graz had been larger and more important than the one in Linz, which only employed a rector, a co-rector, and four professors.

When he assumed the throne, Matthias granted Kepler an annual salary of three hundred gulden, which would continue to be paid after he left Prague. At the emperor's request, he was required to return to Prague occasionally. He was also ordered to complete the *Rudolphine Tables*.

Even in Linz, Kepler could not escape religious conflict. This time it came from his fellow Protestants, and it hurt him more deeply than anything the Catholics had done. It began when a local clergyman, Daniel Hitzler, argued with Kepler over a burning theological question of the time: What actually happened during the Eucharist, or Holy Communion?

Kepler believed the Communion bread and wine did not transform into the body and blood of Christ, a process called transubstantiation. Instead, he thought the ritual was symbolic, a position also held by Calvinists. On the other hand, Lutherans believed in the miracle of transubstantiation. Hitzler asked Kepler to sign a written statement supporting the Lutheran position.

In this French cartoon, the three European religious leaders express their contempt for one another. *(Courtesy of the Bibliothèque Nationale, Giraudon.)*

CALVIN   LE PAPE   LUTHER

When Kepler, sticking to his convictions, did not do so, Hitzler refused him the holy rites—in effect, expelling him from the congregation. This devastating blow to Kepler also created a scandal in his new hometown. He appealed Hitzler's excommunication to the higher authorities, writing, "I have been called a godless scorner of the word of God and of the Holy Communion, who does not care whether or not it was granted, and who, far from being eager to receive it agreed that it be kept from him. I have been denounced as a doubter, who at his advanced age has not yet found a basis for his faith. I have been denounced as unstable."

His request to override Hitzler's action was denied. To add insult to injury, the officials took the opportunity to warn him against combining Catholicism, Lutheranism, and Calvinism into his own personal religion. It was suggested that he concentrate on mathematics and leave theology to others.

Kepler had worked hard for years, beginning with his theological studies, to maintain the integrity of his religious beliefs and to avoid being drawn into conflict. He insisted on his right to keep his religious beliefs private. Religion, he thought, was a personal matter between the believer and God. He had managed to avoid open controversy in Prague, possibly the most religiously complicated city in all of Europe. Now, in much smaller Linz, far from the chaos of the capital city, he was punished for disagreeing with church authorities over a highly specific aspect of the creed. He was convinced his refusal to take sides and more fully commit to the conflict was the real reason for his excommunication. In 1619, he made a final appeal to Matthias Hafenreffer, his old friend from Graz, to be readmitted to the Lutheran congregation. The appeal was rejected with a warning to accept the creed as given to him. He spent the remainder of his life without the official support of his church.

Kepler's religious problems did not deter him from a necessary project he began soon after settling into Linz. He needed a new wife to help with the surviving children and to run the household. He approached the task of finding a wife with customary thoroughness and developed a list of eleven candidates. Then he began a meticulous, and comical, process of elimination. Characteristically, he recorded the entire process in a long letter that has survived and reads like a matrimonial version of *New Astronomy*.

He began by reviewing each candidate for shortcomings that would take her out of the running. It was a long process. "Why has God permitted me to occupy myself with a plan that could not reach a successful conclusion?" he lamented at one point.

He disqualified the first candidate because she had two eligible daughters who would require dowries. In addition, her inheritance did not actually belong to her, but was overseen by a trustee. There was also "a consideration of health, because, though her body was strong, it was suspect of ill-health because of her stinking breath." He next considered one of the daughters of the widow. "I thus transferred my interest from widows to virgins," he wrote, but then decided she was not of "sufficient age to run a household." (The widow was not offended that the daugher was considered, only that she was rejected.) The third candidate was a Bohemian maiden. She had been engaged to a suitor who had gotten a prostitute pregnant in the meantime, which made her available for Kepler's consideration. That complication itself was enough to discourage him. Number Four was tall and muscular, which he did not find attractive. He might have married her anyway, but she grew tired of waiting and married another.

The fifth prospect, Susanna, who would eventually win this bizarre competition, "had the advantage through her love, and her promise to be modest, thrifty, diligent, and to love her stepchildren." Initially, though, he was so upset over the loss of the fourth (tall and muscular) candidate, Kepler could generate little feeling for Susanna. He moved on to the sixth, who was recommended by his stepdaughter. At first she seemed to be the one, but several discouraging factors developed: The wedding would have been very expensive, he felt she was too young, and her noble rank might have made her overly proud and difficult to handle. He did not want a repeat of his first marriage. As he began to return his attention to Susanna, number seven appeared and momentarily distracted him, but not enough for him to propose. Number eight was a commoner who was even more fickle than Kepler—she changed from yes to no and back seven times. Number nine came highly recommended but suffered from a lung disease. He pretended to love another so that he could be rid of her.

Number ten was also a member of the nobility— wealthy and thrifty—but "the contrast of our bodies was most conspicuous: I thin, dried-up and meager; she, short and fat, and coming from a family distinguished by redundant obesity." The eleventh and last candidate had some good qualities, but after waiting months for her answer to his inquiries, he decided she was not mature enough for marriage. Finally, he returned his affection to the fifth, Susanna Reutinger, whom he realized was the most sincere and devoted.

During the entire procedure, he had considered his primary criteria for choosing a wife to be social class and monetary wealth. In the end, he married a woman who had no rank, money, or family. In his blundering way, however, he succeeded. This marriage was much happier than his first. Twenty-four-year-old Susanna was the daughter of a cabinetmaker. She had been orphaned as a child and a baroness adopted her. Kepler met her while visiting the baroness. The two were married in October 1613, not without some controversy. His step-daughter, Regina, wanted him to have a more aristocratic bride. She also considered Susanna too young to raise his two surviving children—Susanna, age eleven, and Ludwig, age six.

Kepler persevered and went through with the wedding. Later, Regina had the good grace to admit she had been wrong. Kepler and Susanna had six children together. The first three died in childhood. Margareta, born in 1615, died in 1617 of cough and consumption. Katherine, born in 1617, died in 1618 of the same illnesses. Sebald, born in 1619, died in 1623 of small-pox. The other three survived. Cordula was born in 1621, Fridmar in 1623, and Hildebert in 1625. Hildebert was named after an eleventh-century religious author who had instructed on Holy Communion and had coined the term "transubstantiation."

CHAPTER EIGHT
HARMONIES AND DISSONANCES

The move from Vienna, death of his first wife, remarriage, and conflict with his church distracted Kepler from astronomy for a few years, but he continued to work on other projects. For example, he finally established to his satisfaction, by use of historical records of a solar eclipse, that Jesus Christ was born around 4 B.C. This date is the one most scholars use today.

He also had official duties to keep himself busy. In the second half of 1613, Emperor Matthias asked him to travel to Regensburg, where the Reichstag was meeting, to debate whether the empire should adopt a new calendar. The Julian calendar, named for the Roman emperor Julius Caesar was adopted by the Romans in 46 B.C. The Council of Nicea in 325 declared that Easter was to be celebrated on the first Sunday after the first full moon of spring and developed a method of determining when that would be. This decree was dependent on having an accurate date established for the beginning of spring, or the vernal equinox.

The difficulty arose because the Julian calendar measured the year to be 365 and one-quarter days. In order to account for the quarter day, an extra day was added every four years, or leap year. Adding the extra day actually made the year too long by approximately eleven minutes. Therefore, over the course of several decades, the accumulated minutes resulted in an extra, unaccounted-for day.

In 1582, Pope Gregory XIII ordered a more precise calendar to be drawn up. In order to push the calendar days back to better coincide with the seasons, the new calendar omitted ten days from October of that year— October 15 would come directly after October 4. The rules for leap years also changed. A year would be considered a leap year if it was divisible by four, except for years which are divisible by 100 and not divisible by 400. The extra day in a leap year would now follow February 28. These changes would help stabilize the date of the vernal equinox, which would now fall between March 19 and 22. This revised calendar, known as the Gregorian Calendar, after Pope Gregory, is the calendar used by Western countries today.

The Gregorian Calendar, which was submitted to all the European states for approval, became an immediate source of conflict. Protestant ministers and princes, jealous of any papal influence, rejected it. Although he was a Protestant, Kepler was sent to the Reichstag to argue for the papal calendar reforms. During the summer of meetings, he argued clearly, moderately—and unsuccessfully—for the changes. The Protestant princes did not accept the new calendar until 1700, eighty-seven years after the conference.

Kepler attended the Reichstag from July to October 1613. In October, he returned to Linz to be married. That year, autumn was beautiful and the grape harvest was abundant. While he traveled home by boat, the Danube River, which runs west to east across Germany, was busy with barges filled with wine casks. As he watched the wine casks being loaded on the barge, he began to think about how the wine was priced. The amount of wine in each cask was determined by inserting a measuring rod through the opening used to fill it. The dealer then read the depth of the wine off the measuring stick and determined the price based on a scale.

How accurate was this procedure? The casks were bowed and not always of a uniform size. How could you determine if the measuring stick provided an accurate measure of the amount sold? The only way to answer the question was to devise a way to measure curved surfaces. After his wedding in Linz, he worked at a solution by rotating a conic section along various lines on a plane and came up with ninety-two different types of curved designs. He then measured the volumes of the shapes and determined that the Austrian cask was the best designed container to provide accurate readings using a measuring rod. In the process, he made a step toward the invention of integral calculus, which allows for the measurement of constantly changing quantities.

Kepler detailed his work in *Art of Measurement*. When it was completed, he began to look for a printer, but there was none in Linz. He eventually persuaded a printer, Johannes Planck, to move to Linz, and together they set up shop. Released in German and Latin, *Art of Measurement* was their first book.

Kepler hoped the work on the calendar and the book on measurement, both of which had practical uses, would placate the government officials who were pressuring him to spend less time on research and theory and more time completing the *Rudolphine Tables*. In 1614, he did return to work on the *Rudolphine Tables* and also began to publish ephemerides—annual catalogs of the daily positions of the Sun, Moon, and planets. These served as preliminary work for the tables and provided him income. He also began writing an astronomy textbook based on heliocentricism to replace the current Ptolemy-based textbook his former teacher Michael Maestlin had written years before.

The year 1617 started off badly and got worse. He began to hear reports from Württemberg that his mother was suspected of witchcraft. This was a serious charge that could result in her execution. In September, his two-year-old daughter died; in October, his much beloved stepdaughter, Regina, died suddenly. Regina left behind a husband and children. Kepler allowed his teenage daughter Susanna to move to Regensburg to help his grieving son-in-law. He accompanied her on the trip, and then traveled to Württemberg where he unsuccessfully attempted to clear up his mother's legal troubles.

While traveling, he visited Tübingen and again asked to be allowed the sacrament in the Lutheran Church. His request was denied. He returned to Linz a few days before Christmas, exhausted and depressed over the deaths of his daughter and step-daughter. A few days after his return, his six-month-old daughter Katherine became ill. She died in February.

Throughout his life, Kepler turned to work for solace and to drive away depression. He had been making steady progress on the *Rudolphine Tables* but now needed a more engrossing task. "I set the *Tables* aside since they required peace, and turned my mind to the contemplation of the *Harmony*," he wrote. At this time of personal grief, when the world around him was slipping into apparent madness, he returned to the theme of his first book and what he saw as his life's work—revealing God's harmonious plan.

He had drafted a plan for *World Harmony* in 1599 at the age of twenty-eight. At the time, he felt "carried away and possessed by an unutterable rapture over the divine spectacle of the heavenly harmony." In *World Harmony*, Kepler returned to the ideas in *Cosmological Mystery*, which led to the development of his third law of planetary motion.

Kepler's goal in *World Harmony* was to find the interlocking structure of the universe, which he was convinced could only be discovered by the use of mathematics. What is perceived through the senses as harmony, most noticeably in music, was to Kepler merely a reflection of God's mind. According to Kepler, we respond to music emotionally because it revives a sort of sensory memory within us of the ideal, which is only fully perceptible to God.

In *Cosmological Mystery*, Kepler used the five perfect solids to describe the intervals between orbits. In *World Harmony*, he developed a wider system of shapes that he labeled either "knowable" or "unknowable." "Knowable" shapes could be constructed by using only a compass and a ruler. Any shape that could not be drawn with only a compass and ruler was "unknowable." In this way, he arrived at a limited number of shapes, just as there were a limited number of ratios that make harmonious sounds in music.

The five perfect solids were three-dimensional shapes that could be inscribed inside a sphere, and the knowable polygons were two-dimensional shapes that could be inscribed inside a circle. In Kepler's cosmology, the sphere represented the Holy Trinity, and the two-dimensional plane represented the material world. He then searched for combinations of the perfect solids and two-dimensional shapes that created ratios corresponding to musical harmony. These ratios would be physical expressions of the harmonious relationship between God

Kepler devised this musical notation describing each planet's harmony.
(From Johannes Kepler, The Harmony of the World, *1619.)*

and his creation, and the corresponding geometric shapes would become the building blocks of the universe.

Kepler was not only interested in finding harmony in the universe. He applied his ratios to various aspects of the natural world. It was not until the fifth, and last, book of *World Harmony* that he turned his attention back to the planets. It was a monumental challenge to find harmonic ratios in a planetary system that seemed to thrive on the chaos of eccentric orbits and varying motion.

He began by looking for the relationship between a planet's distance from the Sun and its orbital period and moved on from there. Did his harmonic ratios match the orbital periods of the various planets? Do the sizes of the planets' orbits form a harmonic series? Is the ratio of the longest and shortest distances of all the planets from the Sun harmonious?

The answer was always no; nothing seemed to fit. Then—much as he had made his other discoveries by imagining himself on Mars mapping Earth's orbit—he decided to shift his perspective to the Sun. This way, he could examine the variation of a single planet regardless of its mean distance from the Sun. Maybe there was a harmonious relationship between the extremes. If he had a ratio for this fluctuation in the orbital period for a single planet, he may be able to find a correlation that existed between the eccentricities of two planets or more.

A planet is said to be at *perihelion* when it is closest to the Sun, and at *aphelion* when at its greatest distance from the Sun. Kepler discovered that the ratio between Saturn at its perihelion and aphelion was 4:5—the major sixth in musical notation.

Further calculations convinced him that he had uncovered a multi-level system of planetary harmony that applied to the planets both individually and as a group. Soon he was describing the known planets as a choir, with each planet having a voice. "The heavenly motions are nothing but a continuous song for several voices (perceived by the intellect, not by the ear)."

In the midst of his jubilation over discovering the music of the spheres, Kepler discovered this simple ratio: The square of the orbital period is proportional to the cube of the mean distance from the Sun. He had, again, almost stumbled on a law of planetary motion. Kepler's third law of planetary motion established a

KEPLER'S THIRD LAW OF PLANETARY MOTION

The time taken by a planet to complete one orbit is called its orbital period. The third law describes the proportional relationship between time—orbital period—and distance, defined as the semi-major axis. The semi-major axis is half of the longest distance across an eclipse.

The farther away a planet is from the Sun, the longer its orbital period. By the time Kepler developed his third law, orbital periods had been understood for centuries. Values for relative planetary distances had to be determined from Tycho's data.

The chart below uses data from the six known planets in Kepler's day to illustrate the third law. The first column is orbital period. The second column is the semi-major axis of each planet, described as the Astronomical Unit (A.U.). Earth's orbital period of 365 days, and its Astronomical Unit (semi-major axis), are defined as 1.

Planet	Period	A.U.	p^2	d^3
Mercury	0.24	0.39	0.06	0.06
Venus	0.62	0.72	0.39	0.37
Earth	1.00	1.00	1.00	1.00
Mars	1.88	1.52	3.53	3.51
Jupiter	11.9	5.20	142	141
Saturn	29.5	9.54	870	868

By using Earth's orbital period and Astronomical Unit as the constant, Kepler's third law can be simplified to this modern notation:

$$\frac{period^2}{distance^3} = k \quad \text{or,} \quad \frac{p^2}{d^3} = k$$

Kepler's third law can also be used to calculate the time it takes any object to orbit another object, such as man-made satellites, and to calculate the distance between two objects based on their orbital periods and their masses.

correlation between orbital period and distance. For the first time, time and space had been collapsed into a single mathematical formula. This was even more evidence that there was a single force operating equally on all heavenly bodies.

World Harmony is an odd book—a combination of mystical speculation, intuitive leaps of genius, and brilliant analysis. Kepler's devotion to Pythagorean harmony, and his commitment to searching beneath the physical reality for evidence of God's mind, made him seem too "medieval" and "mystical" for those not willing to plow through his speculations. Galileo was irritated by what he considered to be Kepler's mystical mumbo-jumbo and failed to appreciate how valuable the three laws could have been in his fight with the Catholic Church. Again, just as with his earlier discoveries, it would be decades before the importance of the third law was realized.

CHAPTER NINE
WITCHES AND WAR

Eight days after Kepler completed *World Harmony*, the Thirty Years' War began. Before the war ended, and years after Kepler's death, large areas of Central Europe were devastated and one-third of its population was dead.

The immediate cause of this war was the conflict between Kepler's old nemesis, Archduke Ferdinand, and the Protestants in Bohemia. The fundamental cause was the complicated political and religious structure of the Holy Roman Empire. The overlapping imperial government and local rulers, combined with the mixture of religious faiths, made the Holy Roman Empire ungovernable. The Peace of Augsburg had only slowed the coming of an imminent war. It had done nothing to remove the conditions that caused so much turmoil throughout Europe.

When he was chosen to be Matthias's successor as archduke of Bohemia, Ferdinand consented to abide by the earlier agreements guaranteeing religious freedom. Soon after assuming office, however, it became obvious he had no intention of keeping his promise. He had his sights on bigger stakes than Bohemia, which was only one portion of the Holy Roman Empire. Ferdinand wanted to become the Holy Roman emperor and to return all the faithful to Catholicism. Politically, his support came from the secular and religious leaders of the Counter-Reformation, who demanded he continue his efforts to eradicate Protestantism. When he left for Vienna in 1618, which was once again the imperial capital, to stake his claim as emperor, he left a group of Catholic regents in power in Prague with specific instructions to begin making life difficult for Protestants.

In May 1618, the Bohemian Estates, a Protestant group, called a meeting in Prague to discuss how to resist Ferdinand. When the governing council of regents ordered the Bohemian Estates to disperse, an angry group of Protestants stormed into a meeting of the regents and threw two of them out of a window. Although the men fell seventy feet, they were not killed. The Catholics said they were saved by the intercession of the Virgin Mary; Protestants insisted it was because they fell into a dung heap. Tossing an enemy out of a window was a traditional way to declare a revolt in Bohemia, and this act, the so-

JOHN HUSS AND THE FIRST DEFENESTRATION OF PRAGUE

John Hus, born in 1371 in Bohemia, worked to reform the Catholic Church more than one hundred years before Martin Luther and the Protestant movement. Hus grew up in the wake of one of the first great crises to rock the Catholic Church in Europe  as it began to enter the modern era.

In 1305, under pressure from the king of France, the pope moved his seat of power from Rome to the town of Avignon in southern France. Although the papacy returned to Rome in 1376, another conflict quickly followed, known as the Great Schism. The reigning pope had died, and it was necessary to select a new one. The cardinals wanted to choose a French pope, but the Roman people were afraid this would result in a return of the Holy See to France. The cardinals, fearing the Roman mob, elected an Italian pope, fled the city, and then elected a French pope. They argued that the election of the first pope had been forced upon them by threats of violence. Later, yet another cardinal claimed the office. The Great Schism lasted from 1378 until it was finally resolved in 1417 at the Council of Constance.

During this period of division for the Catholic Church, Hus became a professor of theology in 1398, and two years later was ordained a priest. Hus, saddened and then angered by these events, condemned what he saw as corruption in the Church from his pulpit in the Bethlehem Chapel in Prague. He denounced Church officials and their exercise of secular power, believing they should be restricted to spiritual matters. This and other attacks led to his excommunication (expulsion from the church) in 1412. He continued his attacks, in particular on the selling of indulgences, or forgiveness, by church officials. Hus also supported the translation of the Latin Bible in Czech and became a Bohemian nationalist.

The Council of Constance, which had been called to resolve the papal schism, requested Hus's attendance. The Holy Roman emperor promised he would not be harmed, but when he arrived, Hus was thrown into jail, tried, and—when he refused to recant his teachings—burned at the stake on July 6, 1415.

Five years later, on July 30, 1419, a radical group of his followers stormed the town hall in Prague and demanded the release of several imprisoned followers of Hus, called Hussites. When their request was denied, the angry Hussites threw several town councilors out of the window of the Town Hall. Unlike the Second Defenestration of Prague in 1618, in which the Catholic leaders survived, these officials were killed. The First Defenestration led to the Hussite Wars, which lasted for fifteen years. Although the Hussites were defeated in the end, remnants of the group remained and formed the core of the Bohemian Brethren, which played a prominent role in Prague during Kepler's years as imperial mathematician.

called "Defenestration of Prague," marks the beginning of the Thirty Years' War.

In Prague, the Bohemian Estates formed a government and seized control of the city. Ferdinand began to raise an army to retake Bohemia. The other Protestant states joined in the armed revolt against the Hapsburgs and surrounded Vienna. This temporarily moved the conflict from Bohemia to Austria. Now the entire empire was at war. In July 1619, the Bohemians nullified the earlier election of Ferdinand as their ruler and asked the Protestant Frederick V of the Palatinate (a Calvinist), to accept the throne. Almost simultaneously, Ferdinand was elected Holy Roman Emperor Ferdinand II.

Ferdinand then skillfully organized an alliance with Catholic forces from Bavaria. With assistance from the pope, Ferdinand and his allies were able to lift the siege of Vienna, then invade northern Austria. Linz fell to the Catholic forces in the summer of 1620. The war would last until 1648.

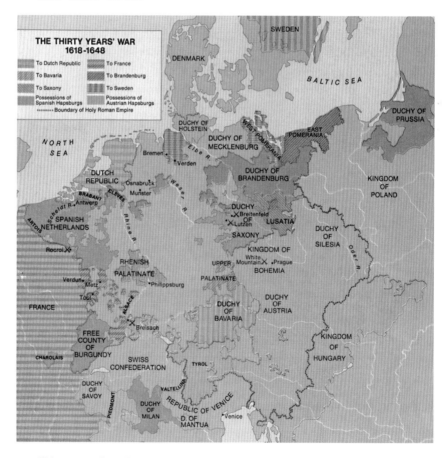

This map outlines the principal areas in which the Thirty Years' War was fought.

Near the beginning of the Thirty Years' War, Ferdinand II was elected Holy Roman emperor. *(Courtesy of the Library of Congress.)*

Once again, Kepler worried about his future under Ferdinand. However, he had another, more pressing item of personal business to take care of. His mother was on trial for witchcraft.

Katherine Kepler had been accused of witchcraft several times, but had always avoided official charges. The phenomenon of witch hysteria began in the sixteenth century and continued into the seventeenth. In 1615, the same year that five witches were executed in a nearby village, Katherine Kepler, who was by all accounts an unpleasant and unpopular woman, began feuding with a neighbor in her hometown of Leonberg. The conflict began over business dealings involving Kepler's brother Christopher, who made the mistake of charging the adversary, Frau Reinhold, with prostitution. When Frau Reinhold became ill from a tincture she drank to induce an abortion, she claimed that Katherine Kepler had placed her under a spell.

Soon others in Leonberg claimed they had felt sick after drinking from a tin jug Katherine Kepler kept for guests. One woman was said to have died, another was crippled. Then it was remembered that Katherine had once asked for a skull that she wanted to turn into a silver goblet for her son Johannes.

The charges multiplied: Katherine had put the evil eye on a child, entered homes through locked doors, and been seen at night riding a calf. The wife of the butcher claimed that Katherine had caused a pain in her husband's thigh by merely walking past him. The local tailor said she had caused his two children to die.

Katherine was her own worst enemy. Nearly seventy, she was argumentative and often confused. She meddled in other people's affairs and had brewed home medicines her entire life. She may have specialized in making a tincture to induce abortions, which would make Frau Reinhold's charge more plausible. Whenever she tried to defend herself, she usually made matters worse.

In late 1615, Frau Reinhold's brother, who had been drinking with the town's bailiff, held a sword to Katherine's throat and threatened to run her through. In response to being assaulted, and in an attempt to head off charges of witchcraft, Frau Kepler sued the Reinholds for libel and assault. This was an almost fatal mistake. The bailiff, a friend of the Reinholds, had witnessed the assault, which meant he would have to testify in court

In the seventeenth century, people accused of witchcraft were often burned at the stake. *(From an etching by Jan Luyken. Courtesy of the Moravská Gallery, Brno.)*

against his friends. To avoid this unpleasant task, he managed to delay the civil trial for months.

Informed by his brother and sister of his mother's difficulties, Kepler wrote the counselor at Leonberg in 1616. He tried to show how ridiculous the charge of witchcraft was. He suspected that his prominence, and role as the imperial mathematician, which placed him in cooperation with Catholics, might have been the real cause of his mother's difficulties. Another reason for him to suspect he might be the real target was that he had once written a short piece of fiction in which an old woman and a demon traveled to the moon. He feared this story had leaked out. The tone of his letter to the court only resulted in angering the bailiff.

This depiction of a scene from the Thirty Years' War shows the hangman's tree, a site for mass executions. *(Courtesy of the New York Public Library.)*

Eight days before the scheduled court date of the civil case, the bailiff finally found a way to bring charges. As Katherine walked along a path, she encountered some young girls. As they passed, their skirts touched. Frau Kepler turned and looked at them in a belligerent manner before going on her way. One of the girls later claimed that when Katherine turned, she hit the girl on her arm, and the girl then suffered a severe pain, numbness, and paralysis in the arm and hand.

The girl's mother threatened Katherine with a knife, insisting that she lift the spell. The bailiff arrested Katherine and interrogated her. When the local barbersurgeon examined the girl, he diagnosed the marks were made by a witch's grip. Frau Kepler made matters worse by attempting to bribe the bailiff with a silver cup. The bailiff dismissed Frau Kepler's civil case and asked the high court to press charges of witchcraft against her.

Kepler wrote letter after letter to the bailiff and the high court. He argued against the evidence, ridiculed the entire concept of witchcraft, and reminded the officials that Frau Kepler was the mother of the imperial mathematician. Nothing worked. The feelings were too strong and the charges too serious for the proceedings to be stopped. When it became clear that she would probably be formally charged, tried, and very possibly hanged, Kepler and his siblings made the decision to whisk their mother away from Leonberg. She was sent to live with Johannes in Linz.

Katherine remained in Linz for nine months before returning home. Back in Leonberg, she moved in with her daughter and son-in-law. Kepler followed her home and attempted to have the original libel suit heard. When this failed, he tried to get her to return to Linz, out of the reach of the local courts. She refused, and Kepler returned home alone in December 1617.

In May 1618, the magistrate examined the witnesses to determine whether to continue with the criminal case. As Kepler saw it, nothing but "sheer old female babble" was admitted by the magistrate as evidence. Between thirty and forty witnesses took the stand. The litigation went on for nearly two years, with the court record covering 280 pages.

Over the next two years, as he wrote *World Harmony* and the Thirty Years' War began, Kepler wrote letters and made petitions to the court to have the case dropped. Then, in August 1620, Frau Kepler was arrested. Because her son-in-law was a vicar—a church official— she was carried out of his house, hidden in an oak trunk to spare him embarrassment, and placed in a cell in Leonberg prison.

When Frau Kepler was interrogated, she again denied the charges. One more interrogation was ordered before she would be tortured. To make her situation worse, her son Christopher, daughter Margarete, and son-in-law had deserted her. The case was becoming too prominent, and they could no longer risk the public embarrassment. They asked that the trial be moved to another city, Guglingen, and washed their hands of the matter. Margarete did write Johannes to ask for his help. Kepler managed to get the trial delayed until he could find a way out of the chaos of Linz, which was about to fall to the Catholic troops from Bavaria. He packed up his family and traveled with them to the relative safety of Regensburg, before going on alone to try to save his mother from torture and execution. He arrived in Guglingen on September 26, 1620.

Kepler found his mother in chains, guarded around the clock. She had to pay for the guards and the firewood they used to keep warm. Kepler began petitioning the court to reduce the number of guards and to have the chains removed.

Kepler assumed charge of the defense. It was soon obvious that the Reinholds had designs on seizing

Katherine's property after they asked the court to inventory all of her possessions. Kepler directed the defense attorney, Johannes Rueff, to write out all the arguments. The indictment had forty-nine charges, ranging from receiving Communion in a Catholic Church forty years earlier, to refusing to look at the witnesses, to never weeping—a charge that Katherine answered by saying she had no tears left.

In August 1621, the defense refuted the charges in a 126-page brief, mostly written by Kepler. Then the plaintiff's counsel attempted to repudiate the defense argument and the entire proceedings of the trial were sent to the law faculty at Kepler's alma mater, Tübingen, where he did have some influence, for adjudication. The faculty, probably bending to popular pressure, ordered Frau Kepler to be questioned under the threat of torture, but then quietly arranged for her to avoid it.

Frau Kepler was taken to the torture chamber, shown the torture device, and presented to the executioner. After the procedure was described to her in detail, she was asked one last time to confess. Although many other victims of witch persecutions broke down at this point, Frau Kepler responded: "Do with me what you want. Even if you were to pull one vein after another out of my body, I would have nothing to admit." She was then led back to her cell. A week later, on October 3, 1621, after Johannes paid the cost of her imprisonment as well as her legal expenses, she was released. She had been in jail fourteen months, most of the time bound in chains. Six months later, she was dead.

After her release, Kepler returned to Linz with his family. While in Regensburg, his wife had given birth to a daughter, Cordula. By now, Catholic forces were in control of Austria. Kepler had been ashamed to tell his friends in Linz where he had been, and most people assumed he had fled the Bavarian Catholic troops. It was even rumored he had moved to England.

Emperor Ferdinand ordered the public execution of twenty-seven Protestant noblemen and civic leaders in Prague. Their heads were placed on pikes for public display. *(Courtesy of the Sammlung Häberlin / Fürst Thurn und Taxis Zentralarchiv.)*

Many changes had taken place while he was away. Frederick of Palatinate had lost the Battle of White Mountain. He and his troops fled and the triumphant Emperor Ferdinand took his revenge. In June 1621, twenty-seven Protestant noblemen and civic leaders, many of whom were friends of Kepler, were publicly executed in Prague. Their heads were left on pikes for public display. Others had property confiscated and were imprisoned.

Kepler found himself in a peculiar position. His conflict with the leaders of the Lutheran church was well known. This put him in a favorable position with the Catholics. Apparently, Ferdinand thought he was a good candidate for conversion to Catholicism, and in December 1621, he made it official that Kepler was still the imperial mathematician. The next year, when "preachers and non-Catholic schoolmasters" were banished, Kepler was allowed to continue his work undisturbed.

CHAPTER TEN
SKYBOUND

In the summer of 1619, Kepler worked with Johannes Planck, the printer he had moved to Linz, to publish *World Harmony*. Kepler was now forty-eight and publication of the book was the crowning achievement of his life. Work continued to provide the best respite from the turmoil of war, the death of children, witch trials, and other human calamities, but his greatest discoveries were behind him. In his remaining years, he created six more calendars and ephemerides. He wrote a short book on comets, finished the textbook on Copernican astronomy he had started before beginning *World Harmony*, and finally completed the *Rudolphine Tables*.

When three comets appeared in rapid succession the year after the Thirty Years' War began, many thought

they indicated God's displeasure. (Comets were tradi-
tionally interpreted as indications of God's wrath.) As
anxiety over the comets spread, Kepler decided to en-
large a pamphlet on the comets that he had written in
1608. In it, he made the point, first discovered by Tycho
Brahe, that comets travel well beyond the Moon. He
described comets as though they were living things and
argued that the heavens are as full of comets as the sea
is full of whales. Furthermore, because Earth and its
living beings are a part of the entire universe, and not
isolated in a separate sphere as Aristotle had believed,
it was logical that comets and other phenomena in the
cosmos could create natural catastrophic reactions on
Earth. There may be floods, mass hysteria, headaches,
and other maladies, he said. However, he refrained from
making astrological predictions of what comets fore-
told. Instead, he argued that measuring comets and
understanding their trajectories might lend evidence of
the future, but that their real purpose is as "witnesses
that there is a God in heaven, by whom all future fortune
and misfortune is foreseen, announced, decreed, regu-
lated, measured and governed."

The title of his astronomy textbook, *Compendium of
the Copernican Astronomy,* is a misnomer. The textbook
was not a survey of Copernicus's system, but an outline
of Kepler's. He extended his three laws to the six planets,
the Moon, and the moons of Jupiter. *Compendium* is
organized in seven books of questions and answers. The
first three books were printed in 1617. After finishing

World Harmony, Kepler went back to *Compendium* and a fourth book was published in 1620. During his mother's trial, he took copies of the fourth book and manuscripts of books five through seven to work on during the long pauses in the proceedings. The last three books were printed in the autumn of 1621, about the time his mother's trial ended.

The first three books dealt with spherical astronomy. He refuted objections to the rotation of Earth. The other four books concerned theoretical astronomy. He explained why epicycles, uniform motion, and circular orbits no longer made sense in astronomical theory. More a handbook for professors and researchers than a textbook for students, it summarized his life's work.

The *Rudolphine Tables*, based initially on Brahe's observations, took nearly thirty years to complete. Tycho's death, followed by the ensuing quarrel with heirs about proprietary rights, and the political and religious conflicts leading up to the Thirty Years' War, were only a few of the hindrances Kepler could point to for the delay. In reality, work was held back by his own reluctance to spend years making the thousands of calculations necessary to complete the tables. He considered it a waste of his talents. To his patrons he wrote, "I beseech thee, my friends, do not sentence me entirely to the treadmill of mathematical computations, and leave me time for philosophical speculations which are my only delight."

At age fifty, he resigned himself to finishing the tables and had them completed a year later. Then began the four-year struggle to have the work printed. First, he traveled to Vienna in hopes of having the imperial treasury, who still owed him unpaid wages, to pay for the printing. Instead of paying him outright, the treasury ordered three separate towns to pay a third of the cost. Kepler visited the towns and collected a fraction of the money.

He decided to pay for the printing himself. But Planck was not skilled enough for the job, which was named after one emperor and would be presented to another, and he set off again, this time to recruit skilled printers. In the meantime, Ferdinand ordered all Protestants in Linz to either convert or leave in six months upon the penalty of death. Kepler was exempted, but another decree ordering the seizure of all books and printed material not sanctioned by the Catholic Church put the tables as well as his entire library at risk.

To make matters worse, the Bavarian soldiers, who had seized Upper Austria for Ferdinand, were billeted in Kepler's print shop. They were growing restless and angry because the emperor had not yet paid them. When the Bavarian commander ordered the execution of seventeen men in retaliation for attacks on Catholic priests, the countryside rose up in a bloody revolt. Beginning in June 1626, the peasants besieged the Bavarian soldiers trapped in Linz. It took two months for the imperial troops to arrive and liberate the town. Kepler wrote that he was saved only "by the help of God and the protection of my angels." He wrote to a priest friend that his house was part of the town wall: "The whole time the soldiers were on the ramparts, a whole cohort lay in our building. The ears were constantly assailed by the noise of the cannon, the nose by evil fumes, the eye by flames. All doors had to be kept open for the soldiers, who by their comings and goings, disturbed sleep at night, and work during day-time."

In June, soon after the siege began, the peasants set fire to several buildings, including Kepler's print shop. All printed sheets of the *Rudolphine Tables* were destroyed, but his handwritten manuscript was saved. This fire, and the destruction of his press, was the final straw. He had long before grown tired of Linz and now asked permission to move further up the Danube River to Ulm, only fifty miles from his old home in Tübingen.

Kepler hoped to finish printing the tables in Ulm, but soon lost confidence in the printer with whom he had contracted. After a quarrel, Kepler left Ulm on foot because the boils on his backside made riding a horse too painful. Kepler, fifty-six, walked fifteen miles before going back and making up with the printer.

Finally, in September 1627, the printing was finished. Before he could distribute the tables, a Brahe heir objected that Kepler's preface took up more space than Tycho's. Kepler had also claimed, on the title page, that he improved Tycho's observations. Because of the agreement, Kepler had to reprint the offending passages.

The finished book was magnificent. The frontispiece (the illustration facing the title page) portrays five as-

The frontispiece to the *Rudolphine Tables*. On the bottom left of the base, Kepler is pictured working on the tables. On top of the stage, Tycho Brahe *(center right)* is pointing upwards and Nicholas Copernicus *(center left)* sits with a book in his lap. *(Courtesy of Owen Gingerich.)*

tronomers—an ancient Babylonian, Hipparchus, Ptolemy, Copernicus, and Brahe, under the dome of a Greek temple. Beneath these men's feet, in a corner, sits Kepler at a small table. He has written some numbers on the tablecloth. A banner beside him proclaims the publication of *Cosmological Mystery*, evidence that his first book remained his favorite. Also on the table is a model of the larger dome, indicating that Kepler was the true architect of the tables.

The *Rudolphine Tables* consisted of tables and formulas that could be used to calculate planetary positions, and a catalog of over a thousand stars. It was also

the first time logarithms, which simplified the calculations necessary to locate heavenly bodies into simple
addition and subtraction problems, were used in a book
of astronomical tables. Because logarithms were a new
invention, he had to provide instructions on how to use
them. He also included a map of the world, with the major
cities located by longitude and latitude.

Kepler had left his family in Regensberg while he
finished printing the tables. Upon the completion of the
book, he returned home broke, unemployed, and suffer-

JOHN NAPIER AND LOGARITHMS

John Napier, the man usually credited with inventing
logarithms, was born to a prominent Scottish family in 1550.
Educated at St. Andrews University, he studied theology (as did
the young Kepler), before leaving Scotland to study in France,
Italy, and the Netherlands. He returned home in 1571, married,
and began life as a progressive farmer who developed various
agricultural inventions. Napier was also a staunch, even radical,
Protestant and in 1593, published a popular anti-Catholic book,
Plaine Discovery of the Whole Revelation of St. John.

Napier's study of mathematics began as a hobby. His work on
logarithms was first published in 1614 as *Mirifici logarithmorum
canonis descriptio* and was translated into English two years later. In
his introduction to the work, Napier explained he wanted to find
a way to avoid "the multiplications, divisions, square and cubical
extractions of great numbers, which besides the tedious expense of
time are for the most part subject to many slippery errors." His
solution was to devise a series of tables that simplified
multiplication and division calculations by transforming them
into addition and subtraction problems. His first logarithms did
not use a base of ten. This idea was presented to him by the English

mathematician Henry Briggs, who visited Napier in 1616 and helped him develop a set of base ten tables.

Although he is best known for the invention of logarithms, Napier also developed formulas in trigonometry and was the first to use decimal notations for fractions. In addition, he invented a mechanical method to simplify multiplication known as "numbering rods." These rectangular rods were inscribed with numbers that were aligned to solve multiplication and division problems. Made of ivory, they were commonly referred to as "Napier's bones."

Due to his genius and eccentric behavior, many believed the mysterious Napier to be a practitioner of dark magic and perhaps a warlock. He died in 1617, having done little to dispel those rumors.

ing from rashes and boils. He was offered positions in Italy and England, but he refused them. Instead, he traveled to Prague, where Emperor Ferdinand was residing, resplendent in his victories over the Protestants. He wanted to present a finished copy of the tables to the emperor and to hopefully arrange for a new position.

The Protestants were in retreat in the winter of 1628, and Ferdinand had named his son king of Bohemia. The emperor and his court had returned to Prague to prepare for the coronation. Many of the military leaders responsible for the imperial victory were in the city. Chief among them was the hero of the Catholic side, General Albrecht Wallenstein.

Although Wallenstein had, like Kepler, grown up as a Lutheran, he converted to Catholicism early in the century. His conversion was determined more by career expediency than religious conviction. After marrying a wealthy Catholic widow, he began buying the estates of banished Protestants. When the war broke out, he financed a large army, and soon made himself indispensable to Ferdinand. By the winter of 1628, Wallenstein was the hero of the Catholic cause; the emperor named him commander of all imperial forces.

Years before, Kepler had cast a horoscope for the general, and when they met again, Wallenstein asked him to revise it. Kepler reluctantly agreed. He knew that horoscopes were often used to influence events, and that sometimes the astrologer was at risk if the predictions were not pleasing. Kepler worked on the chart, prophesying Wallenstein's life up to the year 1634. He ended

---

DEATH OF WALLENSTEIN

An astrologer's prediction might have led Wallenstein to his death. When Ferdinand relieved Wallenstein of his duties the first time, in 1630, the general accepted his dismissal quietly. He said that Battista Seth, his astrologer, had predicted evil men would come between him and his master, but would not cause the end of his career. When Wallenstein was called back into service in 1632, he was again victorious. But soon there were rumors, which were probably true, that he intended to make a separate peace with the French and name himself king of Bohemia. Ferdinand then arranged a conspiracy among Wallenstein's officers, who murdered him in his bed on February 25, 1634.

---

with the prophecy that in March of that year would come "dreadful disorders." (In fact, Wallenstein would be murdered February 25, 1634.)

Kepler became Wallenstein's private mathematician. Although he was not paid by the state, the role did have its benefits. It gave Kepler a powerful ally in court, and Wallenstein was able to claim the great Kepler as his astrologer. He arranged for Kepler to receive a house in the town of Sagan, as well as a printing press and one thousand florins a year. Wallenstein also promised to collect Kepler's back pay from Emperor Ferdinand II.

In May 1628, Kepler visited his wife and children in Regensberg before moving on to Linz to attend to some business matters. Soon he was back in Prague, along with his family, where they gathered before moving to Sagan in July.

Kepler arrived in the new city without many of his books and tools, which he left behind in storage. He disliked Sagan from the beginning. It was impossible to feel at home in this provincial town with no university or culture. He felt like a stranger, banished from the activity of more cosmopolitan cities.

Sagan had been chosen as a refuge for Kepler, whose wife was pregnant with their seventh child, because the town and the surrounding area was predominantly Protestant. He had hoped to live out his life without more religious conflict, but there was no escape. Soon after his arrival, the town came in the sights of the Counter-Reformation. His neighbors were threatened with banishment, the Protestant schools were taken over by the Jesuits, and the churches were closed. Kepler received a personal exemption, but he was filled with anxiety.

Determined to make the best of the situation, Kepler set up a new printing press in his living quarters. The first, and last, book produced in Sagan was called *Somnium,* or *Dream,* which may have been the first ever science-fiction narrative. The work, begun twenty years earlier, describes a journey to the moon and the creatures that dwelled there.

Kepler proved to be a disappointment to Wallenstein, who had hoped that the famous mathematician could provide him with astrological predictions that would give him advantage on the battlefield and at the even more treacherous imperial court. Kepler made several trips to Wallenstein's castle, where he offered vague and unsatisfying interpretations of the stars, but he refused

Kepler was employed by a famous general of the Thirty Years' War, Albrecht Wallenstein, to cast horoscopes. *(From Mathäus Merian,* Theatrum Europaeum III.*)*

The horoscope Kepler cast for General Wallenstein shows the positions of the planets, the Sun, and the Moon, and the date and hour of the general's birth. *(Courtesy of Steinhausen, Deutsche Kultur.)*

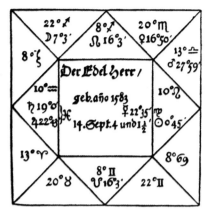

to be drawn into politics. Wallenstein in turn disappointed Kepler when he was unable to collect the back wages. Kepler considered most of the time he spent with the great general to be "a considerable waste of time."

Wallenstein's rapid success had made him many enemies. His power made the other nobles, and eventually the emperor, nervous. In one of the first attempts to rein him in, seven of the powerful electors, whose support Ferdinand needed, forced the emperor to ask for Wallenstein's resignation as supreme military commander in the summer of 1630.

Kepler desperately needed to collect his back wages. In October 1630, he set off to receive a final accounting, once and for all, from the imperial treasury. He shipped every scrap of financial records he could find to Leipzig, where he planned to attend the fall book fair before moving on to Regensberg to make his claim at the meeting of the electors. He knew that Emperor Ferdinand II would also be in Regensberg.

The horoscope Kepler cast for his own sixtieth birthday showed the positions of the planets to be in nearly the same place they had been at his birth. This was a bad omen, a sort of sinister circle. None of his family and friends expected to see him alive again.

Kepler attended the book fair in Leipzig and headed on to Regensberg. He entered the city on November 2, tired and suffering from a cough and fever. At first he refused to rest, but the fever worsened, he became delirious, and was put to bed. He eventually lost the power to speak and could only point, over and over, to his head and then to the sky above.

A Lutheran preacher in Regensberg wrote to a friend:

> He [Kepler] was only three days here when he was taken ill with a feverish ailment. At first he thought that he was suffering from . . . fever pustules, and paid no attention to it. When his feverish condition worsened, they bled him, without any result. Soon his mind became clouded with ever-rising fever. He did not talk like one in possession of his faculties. Several preachers visited him and comforted him with the living waters of their sympathy. In his last agony, as he gave up his ghost to God, a Protestant clergyman, Sigismund Christopher Donavarus, a relative of mine, consoled him in a manly way, as behooves a servant of God.

Johannes Kepler died November 15, 1630, at the age of fifty-nine. The cemetery where he was buried was destroyed during the Thirty Years' War, and the remains of Johannes Kepler are forever lost. The epitaph on his gravestone read: "I measured the skies, now the shadows I measure. Skybound was the mind, earthbound the body rests."

By the end of the seventeenth century, most scientists and philosophers accepted the heliocentric system due in great part to the work of Johannes Kepler. His three laws of planetary motion answered many of the questions left unanswered by Copernicus, and pointed Isaac Newton toward the discovery of the law of gravitation.

Kepler's mystical faith in numbers and his almost religious desire to understand God's universal plan may strike the twentieth-first century reader as being more medieval than modern. After all, while Kepler was trying to measure the space between the planets' orbits with his theory of platonic solids, Galileo used the telescope to discover the moons of Jupiter and the phases of Venus. To many, Galileo, with his faith in observation and experimentation, seems to be the more modern scientist.

But science does not progress by experiment and observation alone. Many of the most important discoveries of the twentieth century were born of speculation and imagination. Albert Einstein, for example, reported that his speculations on what it would be like to ride a light beam across space was central to the development of his theories of relativity. Science is both creative and experimental, and Johannes Kepler used both methods to understand how the universe works. That is why he is often referred to as the father of modern astronomy.

TIMELINE

1571 Johannes Kepler is born on December 27.

1577 Mother takes him to view his first comet.

1584 Enrolls in convent school.

1588 Kepler passes his baccalaureate examination.

1589 Attends University of Tübingen.

1594 Moves to Graz to teach mathematics.

1597 *Cosmological Mystery* published; marries Barbara Mueller.

1600 Begins work as an assistant to Tycho Brahe.

1601 Death of Tycho Brahe.

1604 Publication of *Optical Part of Astronomy.*

1609 Publication of *New Astronomy,* which includes Kepler's first and second laws of planetary motion.

1610 Observes moons of Jupiter through a telescope.

1611 Pubishes *Dioptrice* and *Conversation with the Starry Messenger*; death of wife Barbara.

1613 Marries Susanna Reutinger; writes *Art of Measurement.*

1615 Kepler's mother, Katherine, accused of witchcraft.

1617 First three books of *Compendium of the Copernican Astronomy* published.

1619 Publication of *World Harmony,* which includes Kepler's third law of planetary motion.

1620 Publication of fourth book of *Compendium.*

1621 End of his mother's trial for witchcraft; final three books of *Compendium* published.

1627 Publication of the *Rudolphine Tables.*

1628 Publication of *Dream.*

1630 Dies on November 15.

SOURCES

CHAPTER ONE: Retreat into Studies

p. 15, "remarkably arrogant . . . short-tempered . . ." Arthur Koestler, *The Sleepwalkers: A History of Man's Changing Vision of the Universe* (New York: Macmillan, 1959), 229.

p. 15, "restless, clever, and lying, but devoted to religion," Ibid.

p. 15, "small, thin, swarthy, gossiping . . ." Ibid., 231.

p. 15, "vicious, inflexible, quarrelsome, and doomed . . ." Ibid.

p. 18, "I was beaten," Ibid., 237.

p. 18, "I have often incensed everyone against me . . ." Ibid.

p. 19, "That man . . ." Ibid., 236.

p. 20, "vast appetite for the greatest things," Ibid.

CHAPTER TWO: Cosmological Mystery

p. 36, "[Kepler] was born destined . . ." Koestler, *Sleepwalkers*, 241.

p. 38, "What I could not obtain . . ." Johannes Kepler, *Mysterium cosmographicum: The Secret of the Universe,* Trans. A.M. Duncan (New York: Abaris Books, 1981).

p. 40, "I believe it was by divine ordinance . . ." Max Caspar, *Kepler* (New York: Dover, 1993), 62.

p. 40, "The earth is the measure for all other orbits," Ibid., 63.

CHAPTER THREE: Matchmaking in Love and Politics

p. 47, "simple of mind and fat of body," Koestler, *Sleepwalkers*, 271.

p. 47, "confused and perplexed," Ibid.

p. 47, "not much love came my way," Ibid.

p. 47, "I never called her a fool . . ." Ibid., 275-276.

p. 48, "Everything trembles in anticipation . . ." Caspar, *Kepler*, 78.

p. 48, "every exercise of religion . . ." Ibid.

p. 49, "If only you had sought . . . " Koestler, *Sleepwalkers*, 282.

p. 51, "wrest his [Brahe's] riches from him," Ibid., 278.

CHAPTER FOUR: Tycho's Shadow

p. 56, "You will come not so much . . ." Caspar, *Kepler*, 100.

p. 59, Tycho possesses the best observations . . ." Ibid., 102-103.

CHAPTER FIVE: The New Astronomy

p. 68, "If this wearisome method . . ." Johannes Kepler, *New Astronomy* (Cambridge, UK: Cambridge University Press, 1992), 256.

p. 68, "Who would have thought it possible," Ibid.

p. 72, "I felt as if I had been . . ." Koestler, *Sleepwalkers*, 332.

p. 75, "If you could only preserve . . ." Ibid., 352.

CHAPTER SIX: Fame at the Mercy of Fate

p. 80, "My hungry stomach looks up . . ." Caspar, *Kepler*, 167.

p. 80, "You inquire . . ." Koestler, *Sleepwalkers*, 350.

p. 81, "my mind [is] prostrate . . ." Ibid.

p. 82, "a weak, annoying, solitary . . ." Caspar, *Kepler*, 176.

p. 82, "She would have no master . . ." Koestler, *Sleepwalkers*, 273.

p. 83, "that the heaven does something . . ." Caspar, *Kepler*, 181.

p. 83, "a wonderful emotion . . ." Koestler, *Sleepwalkers,* 356.

p. 86, "doubt, mistrust, challenge . . ." Caspar, *Kepler,* 192.

CHAPTER SEVEN: Chaos

p. 91, "Stunned by the deeds . . ." Caspar, *Kepler*, 206-207.

p. 93, "I have been called a godless scorner . . ." Ibid., 217.

p. 95, "Why has God permitted me . . . " Ibid., 222.

p. 95, "a consideration of health . . ." Koestler, *Sleepwalkers*, 400.

p. 95, "I thus transferred my interest . . ." Ibid.

p. 95, "sufficient age to run a household." Ibid., 407.

p. 96, "had the advantage through her love . . ." Ibid., 402.

p. 96, "the contrast of our bodies . . ." Ibid., 403.

CHAPTER EIGHT: Harmonies and Dissonances

p. 102, "I set the *Tables* aside . . . " Caspar, *Kepler*, 265.

p. 102, "carried away and possessed . . ." Ibid., 267.

p. 105, "The heavenly motions . . ." Koestler, *Sleepwalkers*, 398.

CHAPTER NINE: Witches and War

p. 117, "sheer old female babble" Caspar, *Kepler*, 249.

p. 119, "Do with me what you want . . ." Ibid., 255.

p. 121, "preachers and non-Catholic schoolmasters" Ibid., 258.

CHAPTER TEN: Skybound

p. 123, "witnesses that there is a God . . ." Caspar, *Kepler*, 303.

p. 124, "I beseech thee, my friends . . ." Ibid., 308.

p. 125, "by the help of God . . ." Koestler, *Sleepwalkers*, 414.

p. 126, "The whole time the soldiers . . ." Ibid., 409.

p. 131, "dreadful disorders." Ibid., 413.

p. 133, "a considerable waste of time," Ibid., 425.

p. 134, "He [Kepler] was only three days here . . ." Ibid., 421-422.

p. 135, "I measured the skies . . ." Ibid., 427.

BIBLIOGRAPHY

Baumgardt, Carola. *Johannes Kepler: Life and Letters*. New York: Philosophical Library, 1951.

Caspar, Max. *Kepler*. New York: Dover, 1993.

Davis, Kenneth C. *Don't Know Much About the Universe: Everything You Need to Know About the Cosmos but Never Learned*. New York: HarperCollins, 2001.

Gingerich, Owen. *The Great Copernicus Chase and Other Adventures in Astronomical History*. Cambridge, Mass., Sky Publishing, 1992.

————. *The Eye of Heaven: Ptolemy, Copernicus, Kepler*. New York: American Institute of Physics, 1993.

Kepler, Johannes. *Epitome of Copernican Astronomy IV*. In *Great Books of the Western World*. Vol. 16. Chicago: Encyclopaedia Britannica, 1952.

————. *The Harmony of the World*. Translated by E.J. Aiton, A.M. Duncan, and J.V. Field. Philadelphia: American Philosophical Society, 1997.

————. *Kepler's Conversation with Galileo's Sidereal Messenger*. The Sources of Science, No. 5. New York: Johnson Reprint, 1965.

————. *Mysterium Cosmographicum/The Secret of the Universe*. Translated by A.M Duncan. New York: Abaris, 1981.

————. *New Astronomy*. Cambridge, UK: Cambridge University Press, 1992.

Koestler, Arthur. *The Sleepwalkers: A History of Man's Changing Vision of the Universe*. New York: Macmillan, 1959.

WEBSITES

Astronomy Course by Nick Strobel, Bakersfield College
http://www.astronomynotes.com/

The Galieo Project: Rice University
http://es.rice.edu/ES/humsoc/Galileo/People/kepler.html

Understanding Mathematics: University of Utah
http://www.math.utah.edu/~alfeld/math.html

Viewing the Planets: Cornell University
http://astrosun.tn.cornell.edu/courses/astro201/planet_view.htm

INDEX